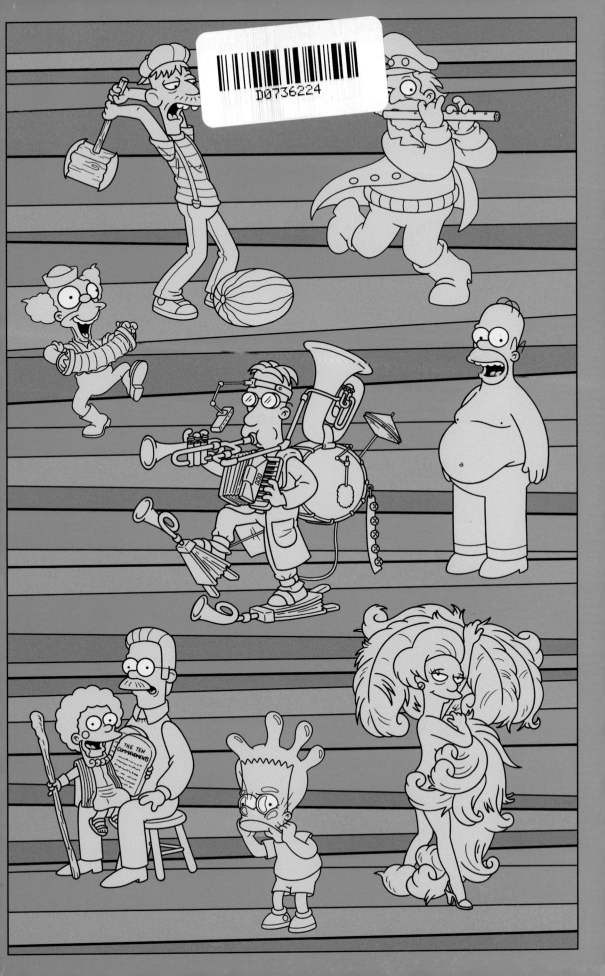

Dedicated to the loving memory of Snowball I:
a feline with great cat skills.

The Simpsons™, created by Matt Groening, is the copyrighted
and trademarked property of Twentieth Century Fox Film Corporation.
Used with permission. All rights reserved.

SIMPSONS COMICS BELLY BUSTER

Copyright © 1999, 2000, 2001 & 2004 by
Bongo Entertainment, Inc. All rights reserved
No part of this book may be used or reproduced in any manner whatsoever
without written permission except in the case of brief quotations
embodied in critical articles and reviews. For information address
Bongo Comics Group c/o Titan Books
P.O. Box 1963, Santa Monica, CA 90406-1963

Published in the UK by Titan Books, a division of Titan Publishing Group,
144 Southwark St., London SE1 0UP, under licence from Bongo Entertainment, Inc.

This book is sold subject to the condition that it shall not, by way of trade
or otherwise, be lent, resold, hired out or otherwise circulated without the
publisher's prior consent in any form of binding or cover other than that in
which it is published and without a similar condition, including this condition,
being imposed upon the subsequent purchaser.

FIRST EDITION: JANUARY 2004

ISBN 1-84023-790-2
ISBN-13: 9781840237900

6 8 10 9 7 5

Publisher: MATT GROENING
Creative Director: BILL MORRISON
Managing Editor: TERRY DELEGEANE
Director of Operations: ROBERT ZAUGH
Special Projects Art Director: SERBAN CRISTESCU
Art Director: NATHAN KANE
Production Manager: CHRISTOPHER UNGAR
Legal Guardian: SUSAN A. GRODE

Trade Paperback Concepts and Design: SERBAN CRISTESCU

Contributing Artists:

EDWIN AGUILAR, KAREN BATES, TIM BAVINGTON, JEANNINE BLACK, JOHN COSTANZA, DAN DECARLO,
MIKE DECARLO, NATHAN HAMILL, TIM HARKINS, CHRIS HARMON, JASON HO, NATHAN KANE,
TOM KING, JAMES LLOYD, OSCAR GONZÁLEZ LOYO, SCOTT MCRAE, BILL MORRISON, KEVIN M. NEWMAN,
PHIL ORTIZ, MIKE ROTE, SCOTT SHAW!, STEVE STEERE JR., CHRIS UNGAR, ART VILLANUEVA

Contributing Writers:

NEIL ALSIP, IAN BOOTHBY, BRENT FLETCHER, SCOTT M. GIMPLE, GEORGE GLADIR, STEVE LUCHSINGER,
TIM MAILE, JESSE LEON MCCANN, BILLY RUBENSTEIN, SCOTT SHAW!, DOUG TUBER

PRINTED IN SPAIN

TONITE ONLY!

MAGGIE COME HOME

BURN HER! *BURN* THE WITCH!

⹋GASP!⹋

SCRIPT
IAN BOOTHBY

PENCILS
JAMES LLOYD

INKS
TIM BAVINGTON

LETTERS
JEANNINE BLACK

COLORS &
ART SUPERVISION
NATHAN KANE

EDITOR
BILL MORRISON

SWITCHED AT BIRTH
MATT GROENING

BART, PUT DOWN THAT *MAGNIFYING GLASS* AND MY SERENA, THE TEENAGE WICCAN DOLL!

FINE, THERE'S TOO MANY GIRLS HERE, ANYWAY! IT'S A *COOTIE* CONVENTION WAITING TO HAPPEN.

YOU HAVEN'T ANSWERED OUR QUESTION, LISA. DO YOU WANT TO *JOIN* OUR BABY-SITTERS UNION OR NOT?

WHILE I SUPPORT THE IDEA, I FAIL TO SEE WHY EIGHT-YEAR-OLD GIRLS NEED THIS KIND OF *SOLIDARITY*.

WE HAVE A DENTAL PLAN.

THIS ONLY COVERS BABY TEETH.

YES, IT FORCES THOSE REPRESENTING THEMSELVES AS THE "TOOTH FAIRY" TO GIVE *FAIR MARKET VALUE* FOR TEETH LEFT UNDER PILLOWS.

I'M NOT SURE.

♪ UNION MEMBERS GET *BACKSTAGE PASSES* TO THE COREYS 2 MEN ♪ CONCERT. ♪

COREYS 2 MEN

OOOH! COREYS 2 MEN!

I STILL DON'T KNOW.

LISTEN, SOMETIMES IN OUR BUSINESS IT'S GOOD TO HAVE "PROTECTION," IF YOU KNOW WHAT I'M SAYING.

YOU MEAN FROM THE MOB?

WE MEAN *PRO-UNION* DOCUMENTARY FILMMAKER, MICHAEL MOORE!

AAAH! I'LL SIGN!

BART, DO YOU HAVE ANY IDEA WHY MAGGIE KEEPS CRAWLING INTO THE *AIR DUCT?*

WELL, THERE'S A *SLIGHT POSSIBILITY* SOMEONE MAY HAVE TOLD HER IT LEADS TO *CANDYLAND!*

I SEE HER! MAGGIE! COME ON OUT, SWEETIE!

MAGGIE'S IN THE VENT AGAIN? I'LL NEED A FRESH PACIFIER AND A JUMP ROPE! *STAT!*

PLOOP!

♪ TA-DAA! ♪

MAGGIE! OH, THANK YOU, LISA! YOU'RE *SO* GOOD WITH CHILDREN!

AW, THAT AIN'T SUCH A *BIG CATCH!* I'D THROW IT BACK AND TRY SWITCHIN' YOUR BAIT. GOOD OL' NIGHT CRAWLERS ALWAYS WORKED FOR ME!

PRETTY SLICK! CAN YOU DO ME?

HEY, YOU BETTER BE CAREFUL! REMEMBER WHAT HAPPENED TO THE FIRST TIN WOODSMAN FROM THE WIZARD OF OZ?

THE ONE WHO WENT *CRAZY* FROM SILVER PAINT POISONING AND TOOK ALL THOSE MUNCHKINS *HOSTAGE* DEMANDING TO SEE THE WIZARD?

YEAH!

PFFT! THAT WAS BECAUSE HE DIDN'T HAVE A *HEART*! NOW STRIP DOWN AND HAND ME THAT PAINT ROLLER.

WOW, THE BABY-SITTERS UNION HAS A *LIMOUSINE* PICK UP AND DROP OFF EACH CHILD! I'M *IMPRESSED*!

BABYSITTER'S LOCAL UNION 203

NO, KELLY! IT'S DAYTIME. WE DON'T NEED TO TURN LIGHTS ON DURING THE DAY!

LIGHTS ON!

LIGHTS ON!

YOU SURE LIKE TURNING ON LIGHTS, DON'T YOU? WELL, I GUESS THEY'LL MAKE IT *EASIER* FOR ME TO READ WHILE YOU WATCH TV!

WE NOW RETURN TO "KRUSTY'S REALLY UNCOMFORTABLE COUCH."

MAN, THIS COUCH IS KILLIN' MY *TUCHUS*!

TRY *NOT* SITTING ON YOUR PUPPETEER, FATSO!

LISA, LOOK AFTER MAGGIE, WILL YOU?

"I HAVE TO *BAIL* YOUR FATHER OUT OF JAIL."

PAINTED-ON SHIRTS WENT OVER SO WELL, I THOUGHT WHY NOT PAINTED-ON PANTS?

WELL, THE BIG SHOT *MANAGER* AT KRUSTYBURGER DIDN'T AGREE!

MOM, I CAN'T LOOK AFTER HER. THAT'S *NON-UNION* WORK. YOU'LL HAVE TO FILL OUT A *STANDARD CONTRACT*...

FINE!

...AND WAIT *THREE DAYS* FOR NOTARIZATION.

HONEY, I'M BEGGING YOU! PLEASE LOOK AFTER YOUR SISTER WHILE I SPRING YOUR DAD FROM THE *BIG HOUSE* AND BRING HIM PANTS.

OH, MY GOSH! WE SOUND JUST LIKE THAT FAMILY I SAW ON SALLY JESSE, BUT *WITHOUT THE GOAT!*

≷SIGH≷ OKAY, I'LL DO IT! JUST HURRY BACK!

LATER AT THE STATION...

YEAH, ≷MUNCH≷ I WENT TO KRUSTYBURGER, AND YOU WERE RIGHT. THE SIGN SAYS NO SHIRT, NO SHOES, NO SERVICE. BUT *NOTHING* ABOUT PANTS. YOU GOT LUCKY, SIMPSON!

WELL, ANYWAY, HERE'S YOUR MEMBERSHIP CARD. IT WAS NICE MEETING YOU MEMBER 203-24.

WANDA, WE'VE BEEN IN THE SAME CLASS SINCE *KINDERGARTEN!*

HI, LISA! THANKS AGAIN!

HI, MOM! HI, DAD!

DAD?

I MEAN *DADDY-O!* THAT'S WHAT WE *JAZZ* FANS CALL...

...TOTAL *STRANGERS* OUR MOM BRINGS HOME FROM THE BAR.

WOW, JUST LIKE THAT FAMILY ON SALLY JESSE. WELL, HAPPY SITTING!

HI!

HEY, BART! NO TIME TO TALK! FOOTBALL'S ON!

YES, I'VE MADE THE ROUNDS. EVERYTHING'S IN PERFECT ORDER. OH, ONE *SMALL* CORRECTION.

THE KID LISA SIMPSON IS BABY-SITTING IS A *BLOND,* NOT A REDHEAD. YEAH, SHE'S WEARING A *BLUE* "SWEE' PEA" STYLE *OUTFIT.*

AFTER ALL THAT STRESS, I THINK WE CAN USE SOME CHOCOLATE-FLAVORED SOYMILK.

SOY MILK

THE DIFFERENCE IS THE AFTERTASTE!

ANOTHER *TOUCHDOWN* FOR SHELBYVILLE!

D'OH!

KNOCK-KNOCK!

D'OH!

COME IN!

I'M HERE FOR THE GIRL LISA SIMPSON IS SITTING.

SHE *FITS* THE DESCRIPTION.

TAKE HER!

HOMER! A LIMOUSINE JUST *DROVE OFF* WITH *MAGGIE* IN THE BACK!

RELAX, MARGE. MAYBE SHE JUST WON AN AWARD. NOW THINK, WHAT WAS SHE *NOMINATED* FOR?

WHAT? A LIMO? *NOOOO!*

SO YOU SEE, MS. SINCLAIR, IT WAS ALL A *BIG* MISUNDERSTANDING. IF I CAN JUST GET MY SISTER *BACK*, WE'LL BE ON OUR WAY.

Baby-Sitters Local 203

I *WISH* IT WERE THAT SIMPLE.

YOU SEE, YOUR LITTLE *LIE* HAS DAMAGED ALL OUR *COMPUTER RECORDS.* ALL OVER TOWN, CHILDREN ARE BEING DELIVERED TO THE *WRONG* ADDRESSES. IT'S *CHAOS!*

EVEN IF I *COULD* HELP YOU, OUR RECORDS ARE ONLY OPEN TO *UNION MEMBERS,* AND *YOU,* MY LITTLE LYING LISA, ARE *PERMANENTLY* DRUMMED OUT.

LISTEN TO ME! MY DAUGHTER IS OUT THERE SOMEWHERE, HELPLESS, HUNGRY, ALONE...

WELL, SHE'S WITH THE DRIVER, AND THE LIMOUSINE HAS AN *HONOR BAR* WITH SNACKS...

WAIT! CAN *MY MOM* JOIN THE UNION? THEN *SHE* COULD LOOK AT YOUR RECORDS.

HMMMM...WHEN WAS THE *LAST TIME* YOU BABY-SAT?

I'M SORRY. I FORGOT WE HAD A DATE TONIGHT, HOMER, BUT I *PROMISED* I'D BABY-SIT.

AAAH! THE PEOPLE'S FACES! THEY'RE *MELTING* TOGETHER!

OH, IT'S JUST A GODLEY AND CREME VIDEO.

NAGEL

MMMMMMM... GODLEY AND CREME.

IT'S BEEN A WHILE.

THEN WE'LL HAVE TO *TEST* YOU TO SEE IF YOU'RE *QUALIFIED!*

FRANKIE

I'LL CONDUCT MY *OWN* SEARCH FOR MAGGIE IN THE MEANTIME. DON'T WORRY, MOM. IN THE WORDS OF MY *LITERARY HERO*-- BIBLIOGRAPHY BROWN, GIRL DETECTIVE, "THERE'S NO MYSTERY TOO KNOTTY FOR AN HONOR ROLL STUDENT TO UNTIE."

SKRREEEECH!

HELLO? CHIEF WIGGUM? I HAVE YOUR *USUAL* EXTRA-LARGE HOG BUTCHER'S SUPREME PIZZA AND SUPER-SLAKER-SIZED SODA!

CAN'T TALK! *FROZEN* WITH TERROR!

THAT'S WHAT YOU SAID *LAST TIME* TO GET OUT OF *TIPPING*!

YAAAAAA!

A *QUICK-THINKING* DELIVERY BOY WAS A *HERO* TODAY, SAVING THE LIFE OF OUR OWN POLICE CHIEF WIGGUM BY STOPPING A THREE-ALARM FIRE USING ONLY A GALLON OF BUZZ COLA AND A POUND OF EXTRA CHEESE TO SMOTHER THE BLAZE.

END OF BROADCAST FILLER

ON THE LIGHTER SIDE, THE TEEN *FORGOT* TO CHARGE WIGGUM FOR THE PIZZA AND WAS *FIRED* IMMEDIATELY.

DADDY, I CAN'T WAIT FOR CHURCH THIS WEEKEND! I WISH *EVERY DAY* WAS SUNDAY!

THAT'S BEING *GREEDY*, ROD. NOW PUT DOWN YOUR UNFLAVORED RICE CAKE, GO TO YOUR ROOM, AND *THINK* ABOUT WHAT YOU'VE DONE.

DING-DIDDLY-DONG!

YES, DADDY.

WELL, HEY THERE, L'IL LISA! WHAT CAN I DO YOU FOR?

MR. FLANDERS, MAGGIE'S MISSING...

...AND IT WOULD REALLY *HELP* IF WE COULD LOOK FOR HER IN YOUR CAR.

WELL, NOW HERE'S THE THING, LISA. ALL THE *MAJOR RELIGIONS* OF THE WORLD KINDA *UNIONIZED* LAST YEAR, AND MUCH AS I'D LIKE TO, I CAN'T HELP A *SCAB* LIKE YOU.

LOCAL 666?

YES, NOT THE BEST NUMBER. IF ONLY WE *CHRISTIANS* HAD GOTTEN THERE A LITTLE *EARLIER* OR A LITTLE *LATER*. WE TRIED TO *TRADE* NUMBERS WITH THE *BUDDHISTS*, BUT THEY WOULDN'T GO FOR IT.

BUT I REALLY NEED YOUR HELP.

NO CAN DO, LISA. NOT WITHOUT *RISKING* MY MEDICAL PLAN...

...*AND* FACING ETERNAL DAMNATION. SORRY, IT'S A REAL *STRICT* UNION.

I HOPE MOM'S DOING BETTER THAN *I* AM.

BRAVO, MRS. SIMPSON! NOT ONLY DID YOU BATHE AND DIAPER YOUR CHILD, BUT IN YOUR *EXTRA TIME* YOU HAVE TAUGHT IT TO PLAY THE *BANJO!*

THE REST OF YOU SHOULD HANG YOUR PRE-TEEN HEADS IN *SHAME!*

A BABY? BUT I'M *SURE* I ORDERED A NEW CASE OF *PICKLED CLAMS!*

LOOK, WE DON'T MAKE MISTAKES.

ER, ASIDE FROM THAT ONE *EARLIER TODAY* AT THE WIGGUM PLACE. ANYWAY, I WAS TOLD TO PICK HER UP AND BRING HER HERE.

HEY! IT'S ONE OF THOSE EENIE-BEANIE BABIES! CAN I HOLD IT MOE? I WON'T RIP OFF THE TAG!

YEAH, WHATEVER! JUST LOOK AFTER HER WHILE I FRESHEN UP THIS OLD CLAM BRINE!

WOW! IT'S REALLY *LIFELIKE!*

BATHROOMS

WHOA! THE DOLL'S *ATTACKING* ME, LIKE THE DOLL THAT ATTACKED PEOPLE IN THE MOVIE, "VALLEY OF THE DOLLS"!

WHAAAAAAAA!

¡GGGLP! GLUG!¡

FWAP!

20

RUUUMMMMBLE!

FWEEK!

PLOP!

EXIT

WHAAA? THERE'S NO *WATER PRESSURE*. IT'S LIKE SOMEONE WAS DIRECTING ALL THE WATER IN MY BAR TO ONE PIPELINE. BUT WHY? AND HOW? AND *WHO*? AND...

EL BARTO

OTTO SAVES

ROOMS

GLOOOSH!

EXIT

WAAAHH!

Can't get of that wonderful D

top shelf

WOW, BARNEY, YOU *SMELL* GREAT! LIKE A NEW *URINAL CAKE*!

IT'S EAU DE TOILET!

BRAAAAAP!

MEANWHILE...

BART, I NEED YOUR HELP! HEY, IS THAT MY EARRING MAGIC MALIBU KYLE DOLL?

JUST A SEC!

SO, MR. BOND, WE MEET AGAIN, BUT *THIS* TIME YOU ARE THAT *SISSY*, PIERCE BROSNAN.

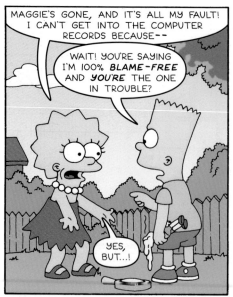

MAGGIE'S GONE, AND IT'S ALL MY FAULT! I CAN'T GET INTO THE COMPUTER RECORDS BECAUSE--

WAIT! YOU'RE SAYING I'M 100% *BLAME-FREE* AND *YOU'RE* THE ONE IN TROUBLE?

YES, BUT...!

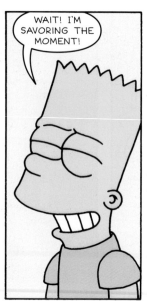

WAIT! I'M SAVORING THE MOMENT!

BART!

OKAY! OKAY! WE CAN SEARCH FOR THE INFO YOU NEED AT MILHOUSE'S DAD'S APARTMENT. HE'S GOT A *NEW* COMPUTER!

YEAH, ALL THE APARTMENTS IN THIS SINGLES COMPLEX GET THE *INTERNET* FOR FREE!

UM...DAD, ALL WE CAN GET IS THIS *DATING* WEB PAGE.

OH, THAT CAME ALREADY LOADED. I'VE NEVER USED IT! HEH, HEH!

WELL, IT APPEARS THAT ONE OF US DOES NOT KNOW HOW TO FILL OUT A SIMPLE *CYBERDATE* FORM.

OKAY, LET'S *CROSS-REFERENCE* THE NAME *MAGGIE* WITH ALL KNOWN SITTER SITES AND RUN A *UNIX SCAN* OVER THE *DOS BASE*.

MILHOUSE, ARE YOU MAKING ALL THAT UP TO *IMPRESS* ME?

YES, MA'AM.

GIMME THAT KEYBOARD!

KLICK!

KLACK!

KLICKETY- KLACK!

OH, MY GOSH! LOOK WHO'S THE *REAL HEAD* OF THE BABY-SITTER'S UNION! IT ALL MAKES *SENSE* NOW!

IT DOES?

HEY, DOES THAT BABY-SITTER SITE LIST ANY *HOT* SINGLE MOMS?

DAD!

WAIT, LIS, I DON'T GET IT.

LET'S GO! I'LL EXPLAIN ON THE WAY!

MEANWHILE, AT BABY-SITTER'S LOCAL 203...

THIS IS KENT BROCKMAN, LIVE AT MOE'S TAVERN, WHERE YET *ANOTHER* MEDICAL EMERGENCY HAS OCCURRED. TWO *ON-DUTY* POLICEMEN STOPPED IN AT THE BAR FOR A *FEW BEERS* EARLIER TODAY, ONLY TO FIND THE PROPRIETOR AND ONE OF HIS CUSTOMERS *SEVERELY* NAUSEOUS. THE CULPRIT--*CLAMS GONE BAD!*

OH, MY LORD! THAT'S *MAGGIE!*

MARGE, WAIT! YOU *PASSED* THE TEST! I WAS JUST GOING TO SWEAR YOU IN!

I COULD USE THE $2.50 AN HOUR, BUT *RIGHT NOW* I'VE GOT TO GET MY *BABY!*

"THE BEST PART IS, THEY'RE DOING THEIR TRAINING AT A *DAYCARE CENTER* THAT PROVIDES *LOW-COST CARE* FOR THE CHILDREN OF *SINGLE WORKING MOTHERS*."

LISA SIMPSON, STOREROOM RAIDER

MUTANTS. *GIANT KILLER HAMSTERS*. I'D BETTER GET *EXTRA CREDIT* FOR THIS.

CRAK!

MISS HOOVER'S CLASS, SPRINGFIELD ELEMENTARY SCHOOL.

WELL, THAT'S THE LAST OF THE *WHITE OUT*. THERE'S NO CHOICE BUT TO SEND ONE OF YOU TO THE STORE-ROOM FOR CHALK.

BUT MS. HOOVER, YOU'VE ALREADY SENT RALPH AND JANEY, AND *NEITHER* HAS COME BACK.

SO YOU'RE *VOLUNTEERING?* GREAT. TAKE YOUR KNAP-SACK AND BRING BACK SOME ERASERS WHILE YOU'RE THERE.

IT'S ODD. I CAN SEE *RALPH* GETTING LOST ON HIS WAY TO THE STOREROOM, BUT JANEY'S A *JR. PATH-MAKER SCOUT*.

AAAAAAAAAAH!!

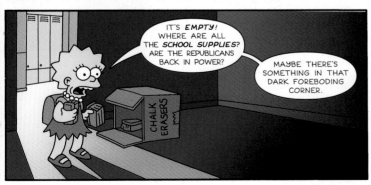

IT'S *EMPTY!* WHERE ARE ALL THE *SCHOOL SUPPLIES?* ARE THE REPUBLICANS BACK IN POWER?

MAYBE THERE'S SOMETHING IN THAT DARK FOREBODING CORNER.

CHALK ERASERS

CLASS!

HI LISA!

WAY TO NOT ESCAPE AND GET HELP, LISA!

YOU'RE *TEACHERS*?

SUBSTITUTES. BUT THE STUDENTS JUST *WOULDN'T* LISTEN, SO WE TOOK THE SCHOOL'S HAMSTERS AND FLED UNDER-GROUND, WHERE IT WAS *SAFE*.

BUT HOW DO YOU *LIVE*?

WE STEAL SUPPLIES FROM THE STOREROOM AND DRINK THE SWEET, SWEET WATER THAT FLOWS FROM ABOVE.

EW! WE'RE RIGHT UNDER *THE NUCLEAR POWER PLANT*. THAT EXPLAINS THE MUTATIONS AND GIANT HAMSTERS.

BUT WHY DO YOU WANT RALPH, JANEY AND ME?

WHAT ARE TEACHERS WITHOUT *STUDENTS*? PREVIOUSLY WE TAUGHT THE HAMSTERS, BUT THEY'RE STUCK AT A *GRADE ONE* READING LEVEL.

Go Dog Go

NOW, WITH YOU ALL HERE, WE ARE *COMPLETE*.

WELL, *I* WANTED TO GET *CABLE* TOO, BUT FREDERICKS HERE THINKS TV IS TOO *LOWBROW*.

MUST WE *ALWAYS* FIGHT IN FRONT OF COMPANY?

DON'T YOU *SEE*? YOU'RE *TEACHERS*. YOU TRIED TO ESCAPE IT, BUT YOU CAN'T FIGHT WHAT YOU ARE.

YOU HIDE IN THE DARK, BUT ALL YOU WANT IS TO SHOW CHILDREN THE LIGHT OF KNOWLEDGE. *FREE* US SO THAT WE CAN ALSO FREE OUR MINDS TO TRULY LEARN.

OKAY, YOU CAN GO.

REALLY? MY SPEECH WAS THAT CONVINCING?

HMMM? OH, IT WAS FINE. THE REAL REASON IS THAT NEXT TO THIS FIRST LAD WE CAPTURED THE HAMSTERS WERE *GENIUSES*.

I CAN ONLY ASSUME YOU TWO GIRLS ARE OF THE SAME INTELLIGENCE.

OH...YEAH. I CAN'T EVEN *REMEMBER* THE LAST TIME I GOT A "C".

THEN ALL IS *HOPELESS*.

SOON...

CLASS. MRS. KRABAPPEL WON'T BE HERE TODAY FOR A REASON THAT I *ASSURE* YOU ISN'T ABOUT A FIGHT WITH MY MOTHER.

SO I WANT YOU TO GIVE YOUR SUBSTITUTE, *MR. FREDERICKS*, YOUR FULL RESPECT.

LOOK, IF YOU RETURN THE CHALK AND OTHER SUPPLIES, I'LL PUT IN A GOOD WORD WITH PRINCIPAL SKINNER FOR YOU.

THE CHILDREN DIDN'T LISTEN BEFORE, WHY WOULD THEY NOW?

TRUST ME.

HE'S A *MUTANT FREAK*!

:GASP!:

COOL! ALL RIGHT! YEAH!

TELL US EVERYTHING YOU KNOW, FREAK MAN!

THE END

STORY
IAN BOOTHBY

PENCILS
TOM KING

INKS
STEVE STEERE, JR.

LETTERS
CHRIS UNGAR

COLORS
NATHAN KANE

EDITOR
BILL MORRISON

RESIDENT EVIL
MATT GROENING

WHO MAKES PUMPERNICKEL BREAD OUT OF DIRT AND MOUNTAIN DEW? WHO HAS A CAR BATTERY IGLOO IN HIS BACKYARD? WHO HAS MISTAKEN PHOTO BOOTHS FOR OUTHOUSES--TWICE? *CLETUS, THE SLACK-JAWED YOKEL*--THAT'S WHO! IMAGINE HIM STRIDING THROUGH THE QUAD OF SPRINGFIELD'S MOST ILLUSTRIOUS LEARNING INSTITUTION. WAIT--STOP YOUR IMAGININGS--FOR WE HAVE IMAGINED IT FOR YOU IN A LITTLE STORY WE LIKE TO CALL...

What Would Possibly Happen if™... Cletus Went to College??

IT BEGINS IN THE LEATHER-LINED OFFICES OF *SPRINGFIELD UNIVERSITY*, WHERE AN IMPORTANT MEETING IS TAKING PLACE...

PROFESSORS BRIGHTON AND MEMMINGER, THE NEWS IS *GRAVE*. THIS UNIVERSITY WAS ONCE A LEAN, MEAN, TUITION MACHINE. THOSE DAYS ARE OVER. OUR BELOVED SPRINGFIELD UNIVERSITY STANDS ON THE BRINK OF *FINANCIAL RUIN*!

THAT EXPLAINS THE FACTORY-IRREGULAR CIGARS AND GENERIC BRANDY.

DEAN, THE ANSWER IS RIGHT IN FRONT OF US! WE SIMPLY *CANNOT* GO ON BEING SO *SELECTIVE*! THIS UNIVERSITY NEEDS REVENUE BADLY. REVENUE THAT COULD COME FROM ACCEPTING THE *LESS THAN ACCEPTABLE*!

HOGWASH! IF THIS UNIVERSITY LOSES ITS STANDARDS, WHAT WILL WE HAVE LEFT?

A GREAT DEAL OF MONEY AND FEWER STUDENTS THAT SMELL LIKE BOOKS.

LATER, IN THE UNIVERSITY CLUB...

SURELY BRIGHTON, YOU BELIEVE THAT EVERYONE IS ENTITLED TO A COLLEGE EDUCATION?

SURELY *NOT!* THE AVERAGE JOE CAN'T POSSIBLY HANDLE THE *INTELLECTUAL RIGORS* OF THIS FINE UNIVERSITY OR THE CRUSHING *LIVER-STRESS* OF ITS KEG-FILLED BEER BUSTS-- AND I CAN PROVE IT!

YOU PICK ANY ORDINARY SCHLUB, SCHMOE, OR EVEN YUTZ, AND I'LL ARRANGE TO HAVE THEM ACCEPTED. THEN, OLD FRIEND, YOU'LL SEE. YOU'LL SEE.

HOW?

STORY SCOTT M. GIMPLE   *PENCILS* PHIL ORTIZ   *INKS* SCOTT MCRAE   *COLORS* ART VILLANUEVA   *LETTERS* KAREN BATES   *OMBUDSMAN* MATT GROENING

SOON...

"...BUT *ENOUGH* ABOUT AYN RAND. STUDENTS, DO YOU FIND YOURSELF CRAVING REAL CAVIAR *TASTE* WITHOUT THE HIGH CAVIAR *PRICE*? THEN TRY "KRUSTYBRAND BETTER BELIEVE IT'S BELUGA-LIKE KAVIAR SUBSTITUTE!"

CLASSROOM COMMERCIALS. BRILLIANT!

...AND THE DEBATE BOYS FROM BROWN BEST LOOK OUT, 'CAUSE *HERE COMES THE COOKING OIL!*

HECK YEAH! KICK THEIR ACADEMIC *#@!!S!!

ROUND 6

ROUND 6

INGFIELD UN

COME FOR THE EDUCATION, STAY FOR THE ATOMICALLY-ROASTED PORK!

GENTLEMEN, AD REVENUE IS POURING IN! CLETUS HAS *SAVED* THE UNIVERSITY!

MMM...AND THIS ATOMIC PORK IS TO *DIE* FOR! WELL, BRIGHTON? WHAT DO YOU HAVE TO SAY ABOUT THE *COMMON MAN* NOW?

MILK
(not grain alcohol--honest!)

CLETUS, I OWE YOU AN APOLOGY. PERHAPS, BY EXCLUDING THE TRULY STUPID, WE DENIED OURSELVES IDEAS WHICH WE COULD NEVER MUSTER FROM OUR HIGHLY ADVANCED, CULTURED BRAINS.

HA HA HEE HA HO HO HA

OH, YEAH. *BRAINS* IS THE BEST PART.

:CHOKE!:

WHAT DID HE JUST SAY?

THE END

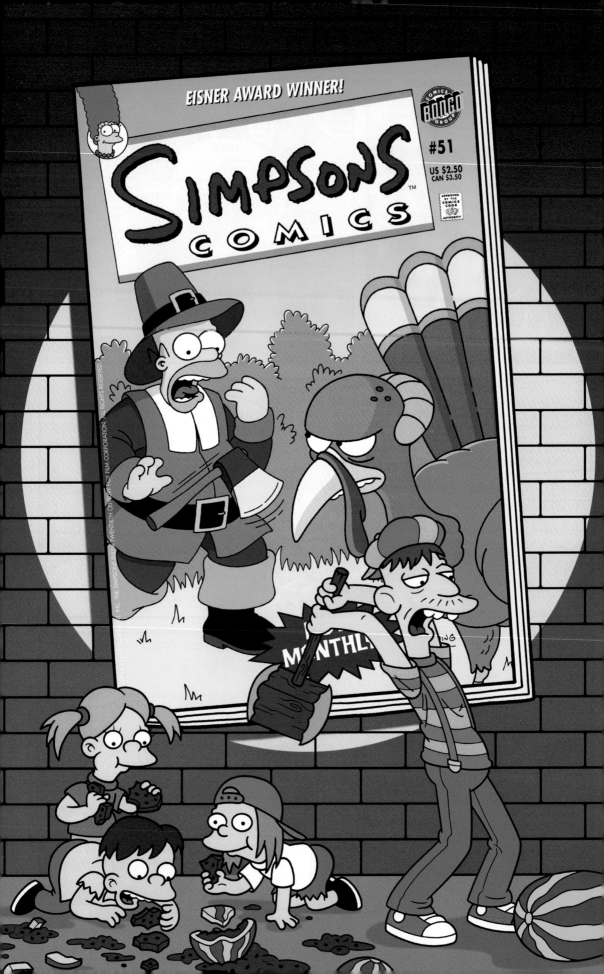

LISA... NO.

BUT, MOM...

I AM **NOT** GOING TO LET YOU RUIN **ANOTHER** THANKSGIVING WITH **PAINFUL TRUTHS** ABOUT THE HOLIDAY!

BUT, MOM...

NO! NO **PASSIONATE** CONDEMNATIONS OF HYPOCRISY!

BUT, MOM! WHAT **ABOUT THE FIRST AMENDMENT**? CAN'T YOU SEE YOU'RE IGNORING SOME OF THE VERY **FREEDOMS** THE HOLIDAY **SUPPOSEDLY** CELEBRATES?

LISA! WHAT DID I JUST SAY?

I JUST WANT THIS TO BE A **HAPPY** THANKSGIVING WITHOUT **POLITICS** OR **TOURNIQUETS**.

WHILE FOOTBALLS FLY, NATIVE AMERICANS CRY AND TURKEYS DIE! THANKSGIVING, YOU'RE NOT

ｇSIGHｇ OKAY... YOU CAN DISTRIBUTE SOME **LITERATURE** AFTER DINNER.

WITH A **TASTEFUL** SLIDESHOW ON THE HORRORS OF **TURKEY SLAUGHTER**!

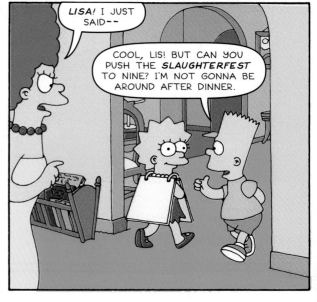

LISA! I JUST SAID--

COOL, LIS! BUT CAN YOU PUSH THE **SLAUGHTERFEST** TO NINE? I'M NOT GONNA BE AROUND AFTER DINNER.

YOU TOOK THE TURKEY OUT OF THE OVEN! HOW COULD YOU EAT *SIXTEEN POUNDS* OF *HALF-COOKED POULTRY??*

IT WAS MORE LIKE A FOURTH OF THE WAY COOKED.

BUT I WRAPPED THE PIECES IN *SALAMI* SO THEY'D GO DOWN *EASY*.

HOMER, WHAT ARE WE GOING TO DO FOR THANKSGIVING DINNER? GRAMPA, SELMA, PATTY, AND MY MOTHER ARE COMING OVER!

NOT TO MENTION MY *BAR FAMILY*, AND MOE, DID I MENTION MOE?

URRRRRRRM...

I'M GOING TO GO GET OUT OF YOUR HAIR AND...

...DRINK.

I'LL BE AT MOE'S.

SUCK! SUCK!

OH, MAGGIE... GRAVY IS FOR *GROWNUPS*.

INDIAN GAMING IN THE CLASSIC ITALIAN STYLE

OH, HOW IT'S GROWN! IT WAS JUST A *TRAILER* AND AN *OUTHOUSE* WHEN THEY OPENED IT.

WHEN WAS THAT?

LAST MONTH.

IS THAT VALET WEARING A JACKET MADE OF *MARBLE*?

SEE 'K' THE ULTIMATE KRUSTY THE CLOWN ADULTS-ONLY EXPERIENCE.

MEANWHILE, AT THE MARKET...

HOLD IT THERE, SIMPSON. YOU WANNA GO IN, YOU HAVE TO SUIT UP.

SUIT UP?

IT'S *MADNESS* IN THERE. ALL CIVILITY HAS BEEN STRIPPED AWAY!

IT'S A *LAWLESS FRENZY OF DESPERATION* THAT'S BROKEN DOWN INTO A HAIR-PULLING, GROIN-KICKING ORGY OF LOW SUPPLY, HIGH DEMAND.

WE'RE HERE TO ENSURE PEOPLE DON'T START *LOOTING*.

I GOTCHA THAT GROSS OF SMALL CURD COTTAGE CHEESE YOU ASKED ME TO LOOT, CHIEF.

GOOD WORK, THERE, EDDIE.

NOW WE HAVE TWO COLORS OF *FLAK JACKETS*, BOOBERRY AND STRAWBERRY QUIK. WHAT'S IT GONNA BE, SIMPSON?

DISCO STU SAW IT FIRST!

IT'S GOT MY FREAKIN' NAME ON IT! READ THE LABEL! IT'S *KRUSTY'S KANNED KRAMBROSIA!*

EXCUSE ME, DO YOU HAVE ANY TURKEYS LEFT?

NO, BUT HURRY OVER TO OUR MEAT SECTION FOR *AMAZING IN-STORE SPECIALS* ON DESPAIR AND HUMAN MISERY.

45

WHILE AT MOE'S BAR...

BEERBEERBEERBE
EERBEERBEERBEERBEER
RBEERPEANUTSBEERBEERBE
EERBEERBEERBEERBEERBEER
RBEERBEERBEERBEERBEERB
RBEERADRIENNEBARBEAUB
RBEERBEERBEERBEERB

MOE'S
DE'STAVERN

NOOOOO!

GIVIN' THANKS AT HOMER'S, GET DRUNK ELSEWHERE.

MOE, YOU'RE GIVING THANKS AT HOMER'S? *HOW COULD YOU DO THIS TO ME??*

SIMPSON, I'VE BEEN LOOKING ALL OVER FOR YOU!

REALLY?

WELL, NO. WE CAME HERE FIRST. YOUR FILE LISTS THIS BAR AS YOUR *HOME ADDRESS*.

HOMER, MR. BURNS NEEDS YOUR HELP. GET IN.

I SUPPOSE YOU WANT TO KNOW WHAT THIS IS ALL ABOUT.

IT ALL STARTED THIS MORNING...

EH...

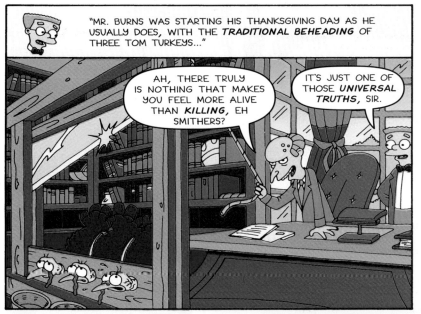

"MR. BURNS WAS STARTING HIS THANKSGIVING DAY AS HE USUALLY DOES, WITH THE *TRADITIONAL BEHEADING* OF THREE TOM TURKEYS..."

AH, THERE TRULY IS NOTHING THAT MAKES YOU FEEL MORE ALIVE THAN *KILLING,* EH SMITHERS?

IT'S JUST ONE OF THOSE *UNIVERSAL TRUTHS,* SIR.

SMITHERS, DON THE PONCHO. DEATH DRAWS NIGH FOR THE TURKEYS.

YANK!

HAH! LOOK SHARP!

WHAP!

DRAT IT! I KNEW VOLVO COULDN'T BUILD A BETTER *GUILLOTINE!*

THOUGH THESE TURKEYS LACK THE VOCAL STRUCTURE TO DO SO...MR. BURNS, THEY APPEAR TO BE *GROWLING.* I BELIEVE WE SHOULD *RUN.*

DAZED AND ANGERED BY THEIR ATTEMPTED BEHEADING, THE TURKEYS *ATTACKED*.

IT WAS *HORRIBLE*, LIKE PROFESSIONAL SQUARE DANCING. IT WAS NOTHING SHORT OF A *POULTRY APOCALYPSE*.

SIMPSON! WHAT ARE YOU DOING?

WHAT DOES IT *LOOK* LIKE? I'M GETTIN' EVEN WITH THAT KID AT THE KRUSTYBURGER WHO SHORTED ME ON PICKLES.

THIS IS NO TIME FOR *MOONING!* THOSE THREE TURKEYS HAVE MR. BURNS TRAPPED IN ONE OF HIS *BRAN PANTRIES!* I NEED YOU TO HELP ME *SAVE* HIM!

OKAY, OKAY. KEEP YOUR PANTS ON.

WAIT--*DON'T!* I HAVE A *BETTER IDEA!* LET'S MOON THAT KID AT THE KRUSTYBURGER!

AW, MAN...A *LINE!* THIS IS *MY* FAULT. I SHOULD'VE SNUCK OUT BEFORE DAWN.

TRY N' SAVE

HEY MAN, PSYCHED FOR THE FULLY-RENDERED RETURN OF *VIOLENT STICKMEN?*

SAY WHAT?

;GASP!;

MEANWHILE...

HEY, ABRAHAM!

ABE.

ABE.

GOOD TO SEE YOU, SIMPSON!

MY MOST *SINCEREST* OF SALUTATIONS, MR. SIMPSON.

DUDE, I TOLD YOU. WHO NEEDS FAKE I.D.'S WHEN YOU'VE GOT MONOCLES?

GRAMPA, HOW DO ALL THESE PEOPLE KNOW YOU?

OH, I COME BY FOR TEN OR TWELVE HOURS *EVERY DAY.*

TEN OR TWELVE HOURS???

WHAT DO YOU DO?

I ALTERNATE BETWEEN EATIN' FRYBREAD, PLAYING ROULETTE,

AND PASSING OUT FROM SMOKE INHALATION.

WHEN YOU CASH YOUR SOCIAL SECURITY CHECK HERE, YOU GET A *FREE BOLO!* *HOT ZIGGETTY ZAM!* THE TURQUOISE IS SHAPED LIKE A TURKEY!

A *TURKEY?* NOT THIS PLACE, TOO!

HEY!

HAPPY THANKSGIVING

HOW CAN YOU POSSIBLY *SUPPORT* A HOLIDAY THAT COMMEMORATES *THE UTTER DECIMATION* OF THE *NATIVE AMERICAN CULTURE?*

A CALLOUS CELE-BRATION OF GLEEFUL REVISIONIST HISTORY, PUTTING A TURKEY AND STUFFING SMILEY FACE OVER *IMPERIALISM AND VIOLENCE?*

BY *RELIEVING* AS MANY OF YOU OF YOUR MONEY AS POSSIBLE. THANKSGIVING IS ONE OF THE *BIGGEST* GAMBLING DAYS OF THE YEAR.

WOULD YOU LIKE A *SHRIMP COCKTAIL,* LITTLE GIRL? THEY'RE ONLY A QUARTER.

WELL, THEY *RELIEVED ME* OF MY MONEY. LET'S GO GET US SOME *CHEAPO* SHRIMP COCKTAILS!

ACROSS TOWN...

OH, THANK GOODNESS!

RELEASE THE PARMESAN, HAG! I REQUIRE IT FOR MY *SECRET WARS STUFFING*, PART OF MY *THANKSGIVING IN THE MARVEL UNIVERSE!*

YES! WE HAVE TURKEYS!

LET GO OF THE CAN, TUBBO! I GOT A LOBSTER, AND I AIN'T AFRAID TO USE IT!

YES! WE HAVE TURKEYS!

WHA? NO TURKEYS! BUT THE SIGN SAID--

THE SIGN IS WRONG...

HOW COULD SUCH A BIG SIGN BE WRON-- ¡GASP!¡

LISTEN CAREFULLY... I HEARD THEY HAVE A FEW BIRDS LEFT IN THE BACK...I WAS GOING THERE WHEN I GOT INTO A SKIRMISH *OVER BREAD CRUMBS*...I WOKE UP UNDER ALL THESE BEETS...

LET ME HELP YOU--

NO! *MY* FAMILY'S THANKSGIVING IS *DONE FOR!* YOURS YET LIVES! GO...*GO NOW!*

HRRRRRRMMM....

EMPLOYEES ONLY

AT STATELY BURNS MANOR...

MR. BURNS NEVER TRUSTED THE CORNISH. HE HAD THESE SUITS MADE UP AS A *CONTINGENCY PLAN* IN CASE THEY WERE TO SIC THEIR GAME HEN UPON THE EARTH. HE NEVER DREAMED THAT THEY WOULD ONE DAY BE USED AS A PROTECTION FROM *AGITATED TURKEYS*. THEY SHOULD KEEP US SAFE.

MY SUIT MAKES MY HIPS LOOK JUST AWFUL! WHY IS IT SO *BULGY*?

UM, MR. BURNS' SKIN IS AS THIN AS *WAX PAPER*. ER, HE REQUIRES A GREAT DEAL OF PADDING.

BACK AT THE TRY N' SAVE...

STAY BACK! *STAY BACK!* I WON'T JOIN YOUR *BRAIN-EATING MINIONS!*

WE'RE *ORPHANS*, NOT ZOMBIES.

THEN WHY DO YOU ALL LOOK ALIKE?

SPRINGFIELD ORPHANAGE BUYS ALL ITS CLOTHES FROM "OLIVER AND PIP'S ORPHAN UNIVERSE."

WE'RE WEARING THEIR *SPRING LINE*.

WHAT ABOUT THE *PALLOR?*

SO IT'S NOT CATCHY?

ORPHANAGE FOOD IS EXTREMELY *STARCHY.*

NO.

SO... ARE ALL OF YOU IN LINE TO PURCHASE "VIOLENT STICKMEN 3D" FOR THE LOW, LOW PRICE OF $49.95?

NO, WE'RE HERE TO GET OUT OF THE COLD AND LOOK AT TOYS WE CAN'T *AFFORD* TO BUY.

WE WERE *KICKED OUT* OF THE ORPHANAGE FOR THE DAY. THE MAYOR IS HAVING A *THANKSGIVING CHARITY EVENT* THERE FOR *ORPHANED PENGUINS.* WE GET TO CLEAN UP WHEN IT'S OVER.

OH.

AT THE NAVAJAGGIO...

GRAMPA, THANKS FOR TAKING ME HERE.

WHY? *YOU* PAID FOR THE SHRIMPS.

ALTHOUGH WE CAN NEVER TRULY MAKE GOOD ON THE *TERRIBLE DEEDS* WE DID TO THE NATIVE AMERICAN PEOPLE IN THE PAST, IT'S COMFORTING TO SEE WE WILL BE THEIR *SUCKERS, PATSIES, AND LOSERS* FOR THE FORSEEABLE FUTURE...

HOUSE GETS BLACKJACK.

OHHHHH....

...THAT THEY WILL *INFLICT SUFFERING* UPON US, *TAKE RESOURCES* FROM US,

AND THE AMERICAN PEOPLE WILL STILL LINE UP, HAPPILY AND STUPIDLY FOR THEIR *BUFFETS!*

IT JUST MAKES ME FEEL *A LITTLE BETTER,* GRAMPA.

HOW ABOUT A HUG, SWEETIE!

HEY! *MY PURSE!*

PITY ME! I HAVE A *COMPULSION!* YOU CAN HAVE MY BOLO.

INSIDE THE MARKET STORAGE ROOM...

MY GOODNESS! WHAT AM I *DOING* HERE? I SHOULD BE HOME *CANDYING YAMS* AND STIFLING MY *RAGE!*

REFRIGERATOR

≧GASP≦ *THE REFRIGERATOR!*

THE NICE LADY UNDER THE PILE OF BEETS WAS *RIGHT!*

NOW, IF I CAN TIME THIS RIGHT...

TATER TOTS

...I CAN KEEP EVERYTHING *TIDY!*

TATER TOTS

AND NOW, TO THE REGISTER! MY, THIS WENT WELL.

TATER TOTS

TWO MINUTES LATER...

54

PLEASE, MARGE, THANKSGIVING IS ALL I HAVE LEFT!

SURRENDER THE TOM!

ABANDONE EL PARVO!

YAAAAAAAAAAH!!!!

SPRING!

OH, MY...

WOW. THE *CONCENTRATED FORCE* OF MY HAIR IS *INCREDIBLE!* I COULD USE IT TO SEND BOXES UP TO THE ATTIC. MY HAIR IS SO...*SPRINGY!* THANK YOU, *FINESSE!*

I'D LIKE TO BUY THIS TURKEY, PLEASE.

TURKEY? I'M AFRAID YOU'RE MISTAKEN, LADY.

LOOKS LIKE YOU GOT ONE OF "COLONEL CURIE'S *ALMOST* TURKEY." IT'S ACTUALLY A *HORMONE-RICH CHICKEN.*

≑GASP!≑

COLONEL CURIE'S "ALMOST" TURKEY

YOU WANT I SHOULD WRAP IT UP FOR YA?

≑SIGH≑ NO.

LOOK! THE DOORS ARE OPENING!

TRY OURS

KIDS, SPRINGFIELD'S *BELOVED* PROFESSOR FRINK HAS AN ANNOUNCEMENT!

THAT'S, AHEM, CORRECT. ACCORDING TO MY CALCULATIONS, TAKING INTO ACCOUNT EARLY DINNERS, FOOTBALL GAMES IN DIFFERENT TIME ZONES, FLAVINS, AND, GHOOHAYS, THE DENOUEMENT OF THE CHARLIE BROWN THANKSGIVING SPECIAL, THE MOMENT AFTER THANKSGIVING IS BUT *TEN SECONDS* AWAY!

HOORAY!

I'M SORRY, BUT YOU KIDS LOOK A LOT LIKE *PENNILESS ORPHANS*. TO GET IN YOU EITHER HAVE TO BE ACCOMPANIED BY A PARENT, GUARDIAN, OR AT LEAST *A COUPLE OF BUCKS*.

WE JUST WANTED TO GET IN FROM THE COLD.

SORRY, STORE POLICY. HANDS'RE TIED HERE. KIDS WITH MONEY OR GUARDIANS, COME ON DOWN.

WAIT!

WHAT?

HOW MANY OF YOU ORPHANS *ARE* THERE?

AN ORPHANS DOZEN. TWENTY FOUR.

LISTEN, *DISPERSE* THESE URCHINS, KID! I HAVE CUSTOMERS TO ATTEND--

ATTEND TO *US*, BUDDY! I *GOT FIFTY BIG ONES* THAT SAY WE'RE GOIN' INSIDE TO *MONOPOLIZE* YOUR TRYOUT VIDEO GAMES AND FLOOR MODEL BICYCLES FOR THE NEXT *TWO HOURS* AT LEAST!

BUT BART, WHAT ABOUT "*VIRTUAL STICKMEN*"*3D*?

AH, I'M SURE MY BUDDY MILHOUSE WILL GET *TWO* COPIES. HIS PARENTS ARE *DIVORCED*.

DEEP IN THE BOWELS OF BURNS MANOR...

THERE ARE THE TURKEYS, SIMPSON. THEY'RE THE PRODUCT OF *METICULOUS GENETIC MEDDLING* THAT HAS CAUSED THEM TO BE *SUPER-AGGRESSIVE*. THEY'RE 99% WHITE MEAT AND THEY *SWEAT* BUTTER.

MMM... *BUTTER SWEAT*.

CLACK! GOBBLE! CLACK! GOBBLE! GOBBLE!

THIS IS IT. *YOU* DISTRACT THE BIRDS, *I* FREE MR. BURNS AND CARRY HIM TO SAFETY.

THEN *YOU* COME BACK AND SAVE *ME* BEFORE THE BIRDS MAKE ME INTO A PITIFUL PILE OF CARRION, FESTERING IN BURNS' RUMPUS ROOM.

LOOK AT ME, TURKEYS! I'M DISTRACTING TO A FAULT!

SORRY, SIMPSON. SO, SO SORRY...

CLICK!

WHA?

CLICK! CLICK! CLICK! CLICK!

SMITHERS, MY SUIT IS LEAKING *BIRDSEED!*

EER--I'M SORRY SIMPSON, WE NEEDED A *FAILSAFE TARGET* FOR THE TURKEYS WRATH!

SMITHERS! YOU PLAYED ME FOR A *PATSY!* YOU *SOLD ME OUT!*

EH.

MR. BURNS!

SMITHERS, YOU IDIOT! *THE BRAN!*

GRAINS EVERYWHERE--CAN'T ESCAPE!

A *BRAN COLLAPSE!* MUST SAVE *EVIL BOSS* AND *LACKEY* WHO SET ME UP!

WHAM!

HOLD ON, DEAR FRIENDS!

LOOKS LIKE WE'RE *SAFE.* THE BIRDS--

YEEEEEEEEK!

61

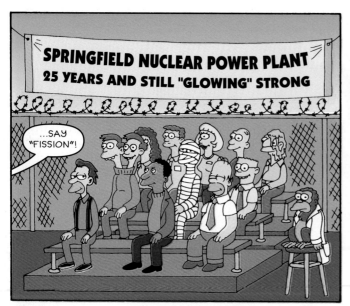

SPRINGFIELD NUCLEAR POWER PLANT
25 YEARS AND STILL "GLOWING" STRONG

...SAY "FISSION"!

I WANTED A PHOTO OF MY *SURVIVING* EMPLOYEES TO COMMEMORATE MORE THAN A QUARTER-CENTURY OF *TRIUMPH* OVER THOSE ANTI-POISON HYSTERIA-MONGERS. AS A TOKEN OF MY GRATITUDE, YOU'LL ALL RECEIVE A WALLET-SIZED PRINT AND FIVE *"BURNS BUCKS,"* REDEEMABLE AT THE COMPANY GIFT SHOP.

CONGRATULATIONS, FACELESS COG.

HEY, THANKS! I'M GONNA GET A TUBE OF *NEW CAR SMELL!*

FELICITATIONS, INTERCHANGEABLE FLOTSAM.

MAYNARD EZEKIEL MC CHIMPY, *WELL DONE!*

I DON'T BELIEVE IT! HE SKIPPED RIGHT OVER *ME* FOR A *MONKEY!*

HEE, HEE, MONKEYS. THEY CAN RIDE *TRICYCLES,* THEY'VE BEEN *ASTRONAUTS,* AND THEY CAN GIVE PEOPLE *THE FINGER!*

SOON, AT THE KWIK-E-MART...

I'M FEELING LOW, APU. GIVE ME A PEPPERONI-FLAVORED SKINNY GINNY, PEPPERONI-FLAVORED SHEEP RINDS, SOME PEPPERONI NUGGETS, AND A SLICE OF PLAIN CHEESE PIZZA.

HELP KRUSTY'S KIDS FIGHT GIGANTISM BIGGER ISN'T ALWAYS BETTER!

WHILE YOU'RE AT IT, HELP KRUSTY!

DON'T EXPECT ANY FREE PENNIES!

I AM AFRAID I CANNOT HONOR THAT REQUEST.

BUT... YOU...ME... HUNGRY.

WE RESERVE THE RIGHT TO REFUSE SERVICE TO ANYONE.

IF WE DO NOT EXERCISE OUR RIGHTS, WE LOSE THEM. SO, I PERIODICALLY REFUSE TO SERVE RIFF-RAFF.

DON'T ANY PENNIES!

I'M NOT RIFF-RAFF.

RIFF-RAFF, SAD-SACK, GOOSE EGG-- IT IS A MATTER OF SEMANTICS.

HUCK'LEBURY HIM EVERYDAY FUNERALS FOR EVERYDAY FOLK

PNB

RASSA-FRACKIN' RIFF-RAFF...RASSA-FRACKIN' SAD-SACK... I'M HOMER SIMPSON! I HAVE DIGNITY!

SPLOOSH!

D' ≥GURGLE≤ OH!

HEY, THAT WAS MY TRASH WATER 'N ROADKILL PARTS! IT WAS S'POSED TO GO IN THE GUTTER! YOU DONE WENT 'N RUIN'D IT!

66

NOOOOOOOOO!

DON'T WORRY. WITH THE DEBTS *I* GOT, I CAN'T *AFFORD* TO CLOSE THIS PLACE. I'VE BEEN GOING KINDA CRAZY ON *EBAY* LATELY...

NEW YORK YANKEES MEMORABILIA...DEPRESSION GLASS...A TRICERATOPS SKULL...A FROCK JOAN CRAWFORD WORE IN "MILDRED PIERCE"...

...AND A COLLECTION OF HAND-PAINTED THIMBLES FROM AROUND THE WORLD. I DON'T KNOW WHAT THE HELL I WAS THINKIN'.

MOE, YOU'VE DONE A LOT FOR US. YOU'VE POURED US BEER...AND YOU'VE POURED US BEER. NOW IT'S *OUR* TURN TO DO SOMETHING FOR *YOU*. YOU GO GET YOUR *GALLBONE* REMOVED, AND *WE'LL* RUN YOUR BAR UNTIL YOU RECOVER. *DEAL*?

WUMP!

DEAL.

SOON...

YOU'RE GOING TO RUN A BAR? I'M NOT SURE I WANT YOU DOING THAT.

ALL RIGHT, THAT DOES IT...

SEE, BART? THIS IS GOOD PRACTICE FOR TOSSING OUT ORNERY DRUNKS.

OUT YOU GO, BOOZEHOUND!

ALL RIGHT, ALL RIGHT! LET ME GO!

MAYBE IT'S A GOOD THING THAT YOU'RE HELPING MOE. HELPING OUR FRIENDS IS GOOD, CHRISTIAN CHARITY.

YES, IT IS...QUICK, BART, WHAT DO WE DO IF A LUSH STIFFS US ON A CHECK?

CHASE HIM INTO THE ALLEY AND BEAT HIM IN THE KIDNEYS WITH A SOCK FULL OF QUARTERS.

NO, A SOCK FULL OF WOOD SCREWS. THEY'RE SHARPER.

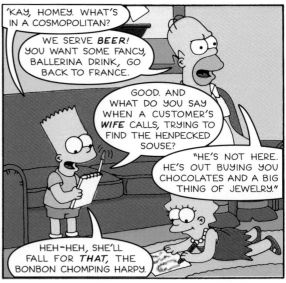

'KAY, HOMEY. WHAT'S IN A COSMOPOLITAN?

WE SERVE BEER! YOU WANT SOME FANCY, BALLERINA DRINK, GO BACK TO FRANCE.

GOOD. AND WHAT DO YOU SAY WHEN A CUSTOMER'S WIFE CALLS, TRYING TO FIND THE HENPECKED SOUSE?

"HE'S NOT HERE. HE'S OUT BUYING YOU CHOCOLATES AND A BIG THING OF JEWELRY."

HEH-HEH, SHE'LL FALL FOR THAT, THE BONBON CHOMPING HARPY.

LOOK, DAD, I'VE DESIGNED COCKTAIL NAPKINS LISTING EACH OF THE TEN COMMANDMENTS. THEY FEATURE MIDDLE-AGED BUSINESSMEN OUT ON THE TOWN WITH SUSPICIOUSLY LARGE-BOSOMED WOMEN.

GOOD. THEY'LL REMEMBER THE IMAGE LONG AFTER THE POINTLESS MORAL LESSON.

THOU SHALT NOT COVET THY NEIGHBOR'S WIFE

AND NOW...

...THE BAR IS OPEN.

OLIVE, CHERRY, OLIVE, CHERRY. GREEN, RED, GREEN, RED. IT'S LIKE EATING CHRISTMAS.

THIS IS LIKE BEING A KID IN A CANDY STORE! EXCEPT THE *CANDY* GIVES YOU A *FALSE* SENSE OF WELL-BEING, AND EVENTUALLY *TURNS* YOUR LIVER INTO A LUMP OF *ASPHALT.*

RING!

HEL-LOOO!

GET BARNEY AWAY FROM THE TAPS, HOMER. AND QUIT EATING THE GARNISHES.

UM...I HAVE NO IDEA WHAT YOU'RE TALKING ABOUT, MOE. HOW ARE THINGS AT THE HOSPITAL?

I THINK MY H.M.O. IS DOIN' THIS ON THE *CHEAP.* I GO UNDER THE KNIFE RIGHT AFTER A DECLAWING AND A NEUTERING. MAN, I HOPE THEY DON'T GET THE CHARTS *MIXED UP.*

OKAY, MR. SZYSLAK, TIME TO FEEL YOUR NOSE, BOY. I HOPE YOU HAVEN'T BEEN *LICKING* YOURSELF AGAIN.

GOTTA GO, HOMER. GET BARNEY AWAY FROM THE URINAL CAKES.

TOO LATE.

HEY, THIS *COOKIE* TASTES LIKE A *PINE TREE!*

CLICK!

SET ME UP, BOYS. EDNA NEEDS HER EYE-OPENER.

AND SO IT GOES...

GIMME A LITTLE KICK STARTER, WOULD YOU, PAL?

SOME HAIR OF THE DOG SEEMS LIKE JUST THE THING ON A MORNING LIKE THIS.

A BLOODY MARY'LL PUT THE WIND IN ME SAILS.

SET ME UP WITH A DOUBLE GREYHOUND--I'VE GOT *CHOIR PRACTICE* IN TWENTY MINUTES.

RUM AND COKE? WHAT GOES IN *THAT*?

WE'RE OUT OF PRETZELS.

NO PROBLEMO. I'LL TWIST UP SOME BROWN PIPE-CLEANERS.

IT'S SO BUSY! I DON'T KNOW IF WE CAN KEEP UP! I WONDER WHAT MOE WOULD DO?

QUIT *DAYDREAMIN'* GLASSES, BEFORE I *RIP* OUT YOUR SPINE AND *STRANGLE* YOU WITH IT. AND *SUGAR-FROST* THOSE DAIQUIRI GLASSES.

...THEN *MAYOR QUIMBY* DROPPED IN TO DISCUSS FISCAL POLICY WITH A *KEY* CONSTITUENT.

KENT BROCKMAN GOT INTO A *SPIRITED* DEBATE ABOUT AN ISSUE OF THE DAY.

AND IN CASE ANY TROUBLE BROKE OUT, *CHIEF WIGGUM* WAS THERE TO KEEP AN EYE ON THINGS.

WOW, YOU'VE NEVER BEEN *SO* IN TOUCH WITH THE *CIVIC LIFE* OF OUR COMMUNITY BEFORE. YOU'RE AN *IMPORTANT PERSON*.

I'LL TELL YOU WHO I AM, MARGE. *WE, THE PEOPLE!*

ME, THE PEOPLE...

ME, THE *PERSON*...

UMM...*HOMER*, THE PERSON...

I'M A *BIG DEAL*, MARGE! LET'S GO UPSTAIRS!

ONE WEEK LATER...

SO I'LL MEET YOU AT YOUR PLACE AT EIGHT ⋮BURP!⋮ O'CLOCK.

"WHEN I WAS A BOY, 'TWAS THE BACK O' TH' HAND AN' THE SOWL O' TH' FUT TO THE LA-AD THAT PUT HIS SPOON FIRST INTO THE STIRABOUT." ANYWAY, THAT'S WHAT *MR. DOOLEY* SAYS. HE WAS A VERY *WISE* IRISH BARTENDER WHO DRANK HIMSELF TO DEATH.

HEYA, BOYS--OL' BLUE EYES IS *BACK!*

YOUR EYES ARE *YELLOW*, MOE. AND *BLOODSHOT*.

THE DOC PUNCTURED MY BILE DUCTS. TURNS OUT MY GALL BLADDER'S NOT IN THE *SAME PLACE* AS A SPRINGER SPANIEL'S.

HOW COME YOU'RE DRESSED LIKE ONE OF THOSE OLD-FASHIONED MOON MEN, MOE?

IT'S SO I WON'T CHEW MY *STITCHES*. ANYWAY, YOU CAN ALL GET OUT FROM BEHIND THE BAR AND RESUME YOUR REGULAR SEATS. REMEMBER, *CASH ONLY!*

GEE, MOE, MAYBE WE COULD KEEP HELPING YOU OUT. YOU KNOW, ALL PITCHING IN *TOGETHER*, ONE FOR ALL AND ALL FOR ONE...

I DON'T NEED HELP, I NEED *CUSTOMERS*. NOW BUY SOME BEER AND SHUT UP.

30 SECONDS LATER...

REMEMBER WHEN *WE* USED TO BE THE ONES PULLING THE BEER TAP, FELLAS?

THOSE WERE THE BEST DAYS OF MY LIFE.

MAYBE THOSE DAYS DON'T HAVE TO END. I'VE GOT AN IDEA...

I'M *WAY AHEAD* OF YOU. WE KIDNAP MOE, KEEP HIM IN A TINY, UNDERGROUND CAGE, FEEDING HIM TINY PELLETS OF VEGETABLE PROTEIN....

...JUST ENOUGH TO KEEP HIM *ALIVE*, AND *WE* CONTINUE RUNNING HIS BAR!

ACTUALLY, I WAS THINKING OF OPENING OUR *OWN* BAR, BUT YOUR IDEA'S GOOD TOO, HOMER.

THEY'RE *BOTH* STUPID IDEAS. IF YOU GUYS OPENED A BAR, YOU'D LOSE YOUR SHIRTS. AND AS FOR *KIDNAPPING* ME, THE CAGE HASN'T BEEN *BUILT* THAT CAN HOLD *SZYSLAK*...

...AS I THINK BOTH THE VIETCONG *AND* THE CANADIAN CUSTOMS SERVICE CAN TESTIFY.

WE'LL NEED *MONEY* TO OPEN A BAR.

I'VE GOT SOME CASH LEFT FROM MY BIG "FAMILY FEUD" WIN.

I CAN INVEST MY *DISABILITY SETTLEMENT*. THEY ALWAYS SAID EATING LEAD PAINT WAS A *BAD THING*, BUT *I* TURNED IT INTO A *POSITIVE*.

LISA'S COLLEGE FUND IS JUST SITTING THERE DOING NOTHING. *NOTHING!* WELL, *THAT'S* GONNA CHANGE.

MY MARRIAGE TO *MARTHA RAE* LEFT ME A LITTLE *INHERITANCE* TO PLAY WITH.

THEN IT'S *SETTLED*. HERE'S TO THE OPENING OF HOMER'S TAVERN.

CARL'S HIDEAWAY.

LENNY'S BAR.

LE CAFE SOPHISTICATE DE BARNEY.

"HOW ABOUT A NAME THAT FITS ALL OF US... *THE BEER BOYS!*"

the BEER BOYS

HEY, NICE TO SEE YA.

GLAD YOU COULD MAKE IT. SHARP SUIT.

GOT YOUR REGULAR TABLE ALL READY TO GO.

BONSOIR, MONSIEUR. ÊTES VOUS DU FROMAGE PENDANT DE LA BIBLIO- THÈQUE DU LOUIS JORDAN?

HEY, BARNEY, HOW COME YOU ASKED THAT GUY IF HE WAS CHEESE HANGING FROM THE LOUIS JORDAN LIBRARY IN FRENCH?

I WAS SPEAKING *FRENCH*?

I HAVEN'T SEEN SUCH *GILDED SPLENDOR* SINCE THAT BACHELOR PARTY FOR *BILL "FATTY" TAFT* AT DELMONICO'S. I HAD ONE TOO MANY CIDER SILLABUBS AND WOKE UP MARRIED TO *JACK DEMPSEY*.

THE CHAMPEEN WAS A LUCKY MAN, SIR.

...AND *HE* SAYS, "YOU DINNAE LOOK SO TOUGH." SO *I* PLASTERS HIM WITH A POSTHOLE DIGGER AND LAYS THE SORRY SOD OUT EIGHT WAYS FROM THE SABBATH. NO FOURTH-GRADER WALKS ON GROUNDSKEEPER WILLIE'S LAWN DURING *RE-SEEDIN'*!

WELL DONE. GRASS SEED DOESN'T GROW ON TREES.

YOU'RE IN, YOU'RE OUT, YOU'RE IN.

SPLENDID. I'VE GAINED ENTRANCE TO THE SANCTUM.

WRONG! I JUST CALLED YOU "URINE." YOU'RE OUT. HEH-HEH.

HEY, THERE, LITTLE BART. I NEED TO SPEAK TO YOUR DADDY.

LISTEN, YOU RUMMY, THIS IS A CLASSY JERNT. WHY SHOULD I LET YOU IN?

I'LL GIVE YOU FOUR GOOD REASONS TO LET ME IN.

HEY, HOMER, NICE PLACE YOU GOT HERE. NOBODY'S PASSED OUT IN THEIR OWN SICK OR NOTHIN'.

WELL, WELL, IF IT ISN'T MOE, THE GUY WHO SAID I'D LOSE MY SHIRT. I STILL HAVE MY SHIRT, MOE, AND I'M GOING TO BUY MORE SHIRTS.

I'M GOING TO BUY A SHIRT MADE OF SOLID GOLD. AND GOLD MOTH BALLS, TO KEEP IT NICE.

AH, IT'S GREAT TO SEE YOU DOING SO WELL, HOMER. IT'S OBVIOUS YOU'VE NEVER BEEN SO HAPPY OR FULFILLED IN YOUR ENTIRE LIFE. AND WHAT I'D LIKE TO SUGGEST IS THAT YOU QUIT IT.

OH, I GET IT. RUNNING SCARED, EH?

SCARED? I AIN'T NEVER BEEN SCARED IN MY LIFE. EXCEPT BY THOSE STICK PEOPLE IN "BLAIR WITCH," AND I WAS GONNA THROW THOSE PANTS AWAY, ANYHOW. BUT IF YOU DON'T WANT TO QUIT ALL NICE AND PEACEFUL-LIKE, I CAN PLAY IT THAT WAY, TOO.

HERE'S THE THING. I CAN'T EVEN AFFORD TO HAVE YOUR LEGS BUSTED. ON TOP OF THE FEE, I GOTTA PAY SOCIAL SECURITY, WORKMAN'S COMP, AND ON AND ON.

SO I'M THINKIN', I PAY YOU GUYS *HALF* OF WHAT IT'D COST TO SMASH YOUR DRINKIN' HANDS, AND YOU *QUIT* THE BEER BOYS AND COME BACK TO MY PLACE.

GREAT TO BE BACK, MOE.

YEAH. I DON'T KNOW WHY WE EVER WANTED TO BE PART OF THE BEER BOYS IN THE FIRST PLACE.

BACK AT "THE BEER BOYS"...

¡MIRA! ¡YO SOY EN FUEGO!

LISTEN, SWEETIE, I'LL GIVE YOU AN EXTRA FIVE HUNDRED BUCKS, IF YOU LET ME EAT MY BUFFALO WINGS OFF THE SMALL OF YOUR BACK.

HRRMM...

DIS PLACE IS DA TOPS. LIKE A *FIRST-RATE* DISCO IN LONDON, ONLY WITHOUT ALL DA KUWAITIS.

GET A LOAD OF *ME*! I'M GIVIN' OUT *WINGS*!

HOMER, KRUSTY JUST OFFERED ME *FIVE HUNDRED DOLLARS* TO LET HIM EAT AN APPETIZER OFF MY *BACKSIDE*!

HOPE YOU HELD OUT FOR A *GRAND*, MARGE. HE'S *LOUSY* WITH SCRATCH.

LATER...

OKAY, THESE ARE UP ALL OVER TOWN.

DRINK UP, BOYS--MOE'S IS *HISTORY*.

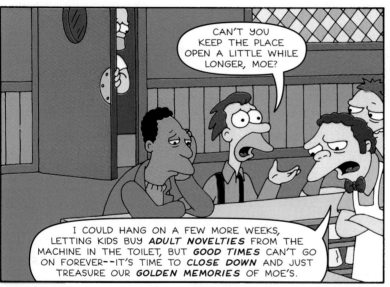

CAN'T YOU KEEP THE PLACE OPEN A LITTLE WHILE LONGER, MOE?

I COULD HANG ON A FEW MORE WEEKS, LETTING KIDS BUY *ADULT NOVELTIES* FROM THE MACHINE IN THE TOILET, BUT *GOOD TIMES* CAN'T GO ON FOREVER--IT'S TIME TO *CLOSE DOWN* AND JUST TREASURE OUR *GOLDEN MEMORIES* OF MOE'S.

GOLDEN MEMORIES...

HEY, HOMER, YOUR WIFE JUST HAD A BOY.

OH, I S'POSE I SHOULD GET TO THE HOSPITAL.

RELAX, YOU GOT TIME FOR *ONE MORE*.

HEY, A QUARTER! TALK ABOUT YOUR *BLIND LUCK!*

MOE, YOUR PIG STINK IS *BACK!*

BUT WHAT ABOUT *YOUR* PLACE?

THIS PLACE IS WHERE I BELONG. THIS IS WHERE MY *CHILDREN* WERE BORN. I DON'T NEED MY *BAR* TO BE A *SOMEBODY*--

I'LL ALWAYS BE SOMEBODY *RIGHT HERE!*

NOW I NEED TO FIGURE OUT WHAT TO DO WITH *MY* PLACE.

HERE, MAYBE *THIS'LL* HELP.

LET'S SEE, I *COULD* COLLECT FIRE INSURANCE. *OR* I COULD USE THE SPACE IN A WAY THAT WILL BENEFIT MANKIND...

SO, YOU WANT TO COLLECT ON YOUR INSURANCE

THE BISTRO

AND AT THE CLUBHOUSE TURN IT'S *DANCIN' MIRANDA*, DRIVEN BY *JOCKO*, BUT HE-E-E-RE COMES *SEXY SADIE*, DRIVEN BY MR. *JIG-JIG!* WHAT A MAGILLAH!

THE END

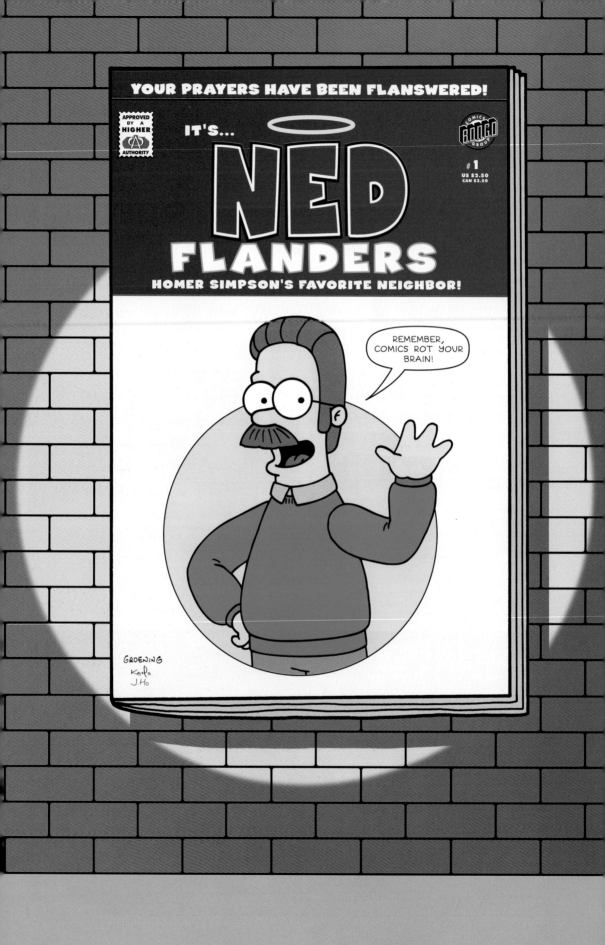

HI-DILLY-HO, NEIGHBORINOS! WELCOME TO THE FIRST INSTALLMENT OF MY BRAND SPANKIN' NEW *CABLE ACCESS TV SHOW*, WHERE WE VISIT THE *HISTORIC LOCALES* OF GOOD, OLD SPRINGFIELD.

Bless this Mess

Around Town
with
Ned Flanders

YOU KNOW, IT WASN'T LONG AFTER OUR TOWN WAS DISCOVERED BY JEBEDIAH SPRINGFIELD-- OL' HEATHEN THOUGH HE WAS--THAT THE *FIRST CHURCH* WAS BUILT USING LOGS, MUD AND THE NATIVE'S TEEPEES.

WELL, SIR, OUR HOUSES OF WORSHIP HAVE COME A *LONG WAY* SINCE THEN, FROM "PASTOR PAT'S REVIVAL HALL FOR THUMPIN' AND HOLY ROLLIN'" IN THE '30'S, TO REVEREND LOVEJOY'S MODERN GLASS SANCTUARY OF TODAY.

THESE ARE JUST A *FEW* OF THE EXCI-DIDDILY-ITING LOCATIONS WE'LL BE EXAMINING *IN FULL DETAIL* ON TODAY'S SHOW!

WITH THE HELP OF MY TWO, TRUE-BLUE, CREW-BUDDIES: ROD, BEHIND THE CAMERA, AND TODD ON SOUND...

WE'LL HAVE A FAN-DIDDILY-TASTIC TIME AS WE SEE THE SIGHTS OF SPRINGFIELD!

YOU BOYS HAVE FUN. I PACKED SANDWICHES!

SO, SHALL WE *FIRE UP* THE OL' FLANDERS-MOBILE?

YOU BET YOUR *BIPPY!* THE WONDERFUL WORLD OF WANDERING AWAITS US, SO LET'S GO!

NOW, THE HISTORIC POINTS OF INTEREST IN OUR FAIR TOWN ARE *NOT* LIMITED TO CHURCHES ALONE! NO SIREE, BOB!

WE'LL *ALSO* VISIT THE UNDERGROUND GRAPEFRUIT GROTTO, THE WESTSIDE SILENT DINNER THEATER, AND THE BIGGEST CAN-OPENER COLLECTION THIS SIDE OF THE MISSISSIPPI...

...NOT TO MENTION THE LOVELY GARDEN OF TALKING STATUES AT THE SPRINGFIELD FUNERAL HOME... *OH, DEAR!*

HEY!

DADDY! LOOK OUT!

JIMMINY CRICKET!

SCREEEECH!

THUMP!

GOOD HEAVENS! *WHAT* HAVE I DONE?

IS IT *LEVIATHAN* CAST FROM THE SEA, DADDY?

GEE, I'M SORRY MISTER, I DIDN'T EVEN *KNOW* SHE WAS YOUR GAL...

DADDY, HE SMELLS LIKE THE OUTDOOR *POTTY* AT YOUTH CAMP!

NEVER MIND, TODD. :UMPH!: HE'S STILL ONE OF :AHMPH!: GOD'S CREATURES AND NEEDS :OOPH!: *MEDICAL ATTENTION!*

'SIDES, SHE TALKED TO *ME* FIRST...

NOW WHEN WE GET TO THE HOSPITAL, YOU BOYS LET *ME* DO ALL THE TALKING! I DON'T WANT ANYONE THINKING THAT THIS POOR MAN WAS *IN ANY WAY* RESPONSIBLE!

HEY MATILDA! GIVE US A SMOOCH!

OH, MAMA! COULD MY TIMING *GET* ANY BETTER?

ALL RIGHT, NERD DUDE! *PEEL OUT* AND DRIVE *FASTER* THAN YOU'VE EVER DRIVEN BEFORE!

BOYS, AS LONG AS WE COOPERATE, EVERYTHING WILL BE OKILLY-DOKILLY!

OW!

BUT, DADDY, WE'RE SCARED!

BY THE RULES OF THE *CONVENIENCE STORE CONVENTION*, I PLACE YOU UNDER KWIK-E-MART ARREST! *STOP* THIS CAR AT ONCE!

KA-CLUMP!

YAAAAAH!

YOU ARE A BAD, BAD MAN, MR. *GETAWAY* DRIVER! YOU SHOULD KNOW THAT A HINDU MANAGER AND HIS MONEY ARE NOT SOON PARTED!

GETAWAY DRIVER?? NOW, THAT'S JUST *CRAZY* TALK!

KEEP THE PEDAL TO THE METAL, KEMOSABE, OR I'LL PUT SOME METAL IN YOUR NOODLE!

Springfield P.D. Saturday 03/06 10:17 a.m.

WHOO-A! WHOO-A! WHOO-A!

LOOKS LIKE WE GOT US SOME *JOY RIDERS* HERE, LOU!

LET'S BRING 'EM DOWN A FEW NOTCHES.

YOU SAID IT, CHIEF!

WHOO-A! WHOO-A! WHOO-A!

BANG!

BANG!

DADDY, I THINK THE POLICE ARE *SHOOTING* AT US...

WHAT??! TH-THAT'S RI-DIDDILY-DICULOUS! H-HAVE THEY GONE *INSANE*?

LOOK OUT, LITTLE NERD DUDE!

...OOOOH!

BUMP!

BANG!

HEINOUS! I SHOT OUT THE TIRE OF MY *OWN* GETAWAY CAR!

HSSSSSSSS!

Springfield P.D. Saturday 03/06 10:20 a.m.

WHOO-A! WHOO-A! WHOO-A!

WE GOT 'EM NOW, LOU. THEY'VE LOST CONTROL OF THEIR VEHICLE! COME TA POPPA, YOU SCOFFLAWS!

YEAH, BUT CHIEF, IF YOU DON'T *SLOW* DOWN, WE MIGHT...

LORD, PROTECT US! WE'RE GOING TO...

CRASH!

THE FOLLOWING STORY YOU'VE JUST SEEN IS TRUE.

DUE TO ITS GRAPHIC NATURE, PARENTAL GUIDANCE IS SUGGESTED...WHICH IS SOMETHING WE PROBABLY SHOULD HAVE WARNED YOU ABOUT EARLIER...SORRY.

ANYWAY, HERE'S WHAT HAPPENED TO THE INDIVIDUALS INVOLVED...

SNAKE WAS *LOCKED-DOWN* IN A *MAXIMUM SECURITY* CELL AT THE SPRINGFIELD PRISON.

TWO HOURS LATER HE WAS SEEN BOARDING A FLIGHT TO MEXICO.

110968

APU *RETRIEVED* HIS STOLEN MONEY, WHICH AMOUNTED TO $25.17. WHILE THE KWIK-E-MART WAS LEFT UNATTENDED, A DISPLAY CASE FULL OF *FROZEN YOGURT* WAS STOLEN.

ROD FLANDERS HAD *BRIDGEWORK* AND A *MINOR OPERATION* TO REMOVE A CAMERA EYEPIECE FROM HIS EYE SOCKET.

FOR SIX MONTHS, TODD FLANDERS HAD TO BE DOWNGRADED FROM "BIG BOY" SHORTS TO *PLASTIC PANTS* AT BEDTIME.

CHIEF WIGGUM WAS FEATURED ON THE HIT *FOX SPECIAL*, "WHEN GOOD SNACKS GO BAD."

Springfield P.D.
Saturday 03/06
10:45 a.m.

AND NED FLANDERS WON A LOCAL EMMY FOR HIS ENTERTAINING DOCUMENTARY-- BUT REFUSED THE AWARD, SAYING HE COULDN'T ACCEPT ANY GRAVEN IMAGES.

REPAIR ESTIMATE

AL'S TO

END

SCRIPT
JESSE LEON McCANN

PENCILS
PHIL ORTIZ

INKS
TIM HARKINS

COLOR & LETTERS
KAREN BATES

EDITOR
BILL MORRISON

THE END!

STORY
GEORGE GLADIR

PENCILS
EDWIN AGUILAR

INKS
JASON HO

LETTERS
KAREN BATES

COLORS
ART VILLANUEVA

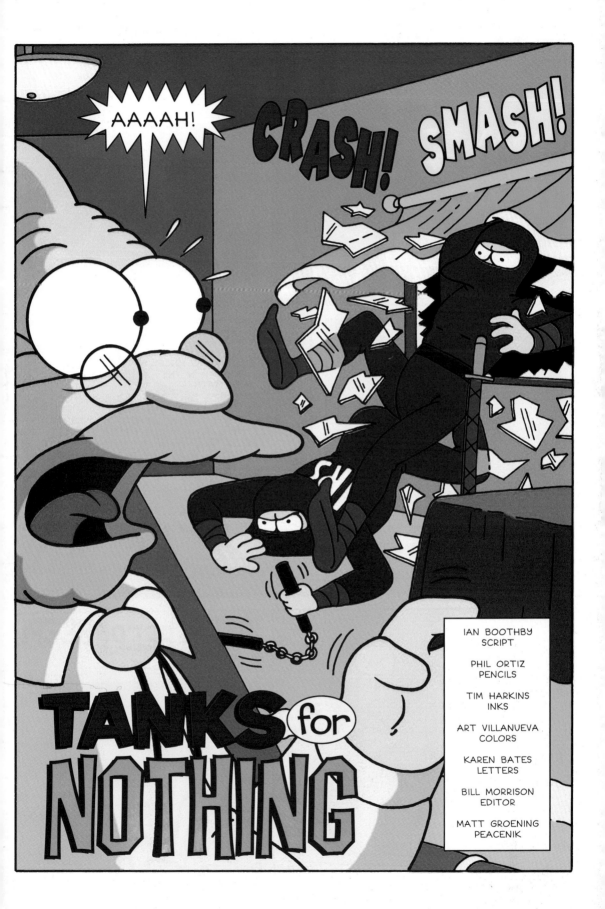

LATER, AT A GOVERNMENT OFFICE...

WELL, MR. SIMPSON, IT'S A *RARE* CASE WHERE A GOVERNMENT AGENCY HAS MADE A *MISTAKE*.

SIR, WE BOMBED THE *WRONG* EMBASSY AGAIN.

I DON'T EVEN THINK THERE *IS A PRUSSIA* ANYMORE.

KELLY, IX-NAY IN FRONT OF THE IVILIAN-SAY!

NOW, MR. SIMPSON, YOU HAVE *TWO OPTIONS*. YOU COULD TAKE THIS *CHECK* FOR THE AMOUNT WE OWE YOU.

GIMME! GIMME! GIMME!

OR...

...WE COULD LET YOU TAKE THE ITEM OF YOUR *CHOICE* FROM OUR *WAREHOUSE!* ALL ITEMS THE GOVERNMENT NO LONGER HAS USE FOR.

NASA

SWEET MOTHER MCGILLICUTTY!

ROSWELL ALIENS
ROSWELL ALIENS
ROSWELL ALIENS
ROSWELL ALIENS

PRESIDENTIAL ROBOTS

SOON, AT CITY HALL...

THOOM!

CUTBACK ON THE *POLICE SLUSH FUND*, WILL YA, QUIMBY?

LATER...

SOON...

EIGHT BALL IN THE CORNER POCKET!

YOU FORGOT THE FRIES LAST TIME!

THEY'RE IN THERE *THIS* TIME, SIR. I *PROMISE*!

KRUSTYBURGER

MENU

WHOA, DUDE! SUDDENLY MY MASCULINITY FEELS *SO* THREATENED.

CRACKLES   CRACKLES

SMITHERS, IS THAT A V-67 *SHERWOOD TANK?*

I'LL HAVE TO DOUBLE CHECK MY TIME LIFE BOOKS, SIR, BUT I'D SAY "YES."

AH, THAT TAKES ME BACK.

MEANWHILE, IN THE NEXT TOWN OVER...

SHELBYVILLE NUCLEAR POWER PLANT

EMPLOYEE PARKING ONLY

FREDERICKS, LOOK AT THE SATELLITE SPY-CAM FEED FROM THE SPRINGFIELD PLANT'S PARKING LOT. IS THAT A *V-67 SHERWOOD TANK?*

I BELIEVE IT IS, MR. AMADOPOLIS.

SO THAT TWO-FACED JANUS, MONTY BURNS, HAS BROKEN THE *ARMS TREATY*.

YOU SEE, SMITHERS, I WASN'T ALWAYS THE *MIDDLE-AGED* MAN YOU SEE BEFORE YOU.

I USED TO BE THE *LEADER* OF A *SPRINGFIELD GANG.* I KNOW IT MUST BE HARD IMAGINING ME CLAD HEAD TO TOE IN *LEATHER.*

I SAY, AMADOPOLIS, YOUR TOWN, SHELBYVILLE, HAS A *WEAK POLITICAL SYSTEM* AND *INEPT SANITATION MANAGEMENT.*

YES, WELL SPRINGFIELD HAS A *MEDIOCRE POST-SECONDARY EDUCATION FACILITY* AND *POOR TAX INCENTIVES FOR THE UPPER MIDDLE CLASS.*

"WE GOT OLDER, ARMIES GOT MORE *PRICEY,* AND *THE SLAUGHTER OF INNOCENTS* LOST ITS *APPEAL.* WE SIGNED A *TREATY* AND WENT OUR SEPARATE WAYS."

WELL, THAT'S ENOUGH REMINISCING. START MY CAR WILL YOU, SMITHERS?

SMITHERS?

MMMM... HEAD TO TOE IN LEATHER.

THAT AFTERNOON...

HEY, HOMER! WE MADE A HANG GLIDER OUT OF PILLOW-CASES AND POPSICLE STICKS. WATCH ME TEST IT OUT!

HMMMM. I DON'T KNOW, BOY. BETTER LET MILHOUSE TRY IT FIRST!

WAR! HUH! GOOD GOD, Y'ALL! WHAT IS IT GOOD FOR?

WE ASKED MAYOR QUIMBY.

KENT

I, ER...AH, HAVE BEEN INFORMED THAT AS OF NOON TODAY, SHELBYVILLE, UNDER THE ADVICE OF ARISTOTLE AMADOPOLIS, HAS *DECLARED WAR* ON SPRINGFIELD.

THERE IS *NO REASON* TO *PANIC*, AND I'LL BE BACK FROM MY *VACATION* TO...AH... UM...WHEREVER...AS SOON AS POSSIBLE.

BLAME FOR THIS IS BEING PLACED IN THE WRINKLED LAP OF MONTGOMERY BURNS, WHO APPARENTLY *BROKE* THE *"NO WEAPONS ARRANGEMENT"* OF THE *"TWO RICH PUNKS TREATY"*.

POINTING THE FINGER

KENT

"SHELBYVILLE HAS RESPONDED BY *STOCKPILING* GROUND, AIR, AND NUCLEAR WEAPONS."

SHELBYVILLE NUCLEAR POWER PLANT

IF IT'S A FIGHT MONTGOMERY BURNS WANTS, WE SHALL SOON SEE WHO IS ZEUS AND WHO IS MERELY ODIN!

I DIDN'T GO LOOKING FOR A FIGHT, BUT IF MY FRIEND *IS* SPOILING FOR A SCUFFLE, I'M JUST THE JAKE TO GIVE IT TO HIM. WE WILL NOT STOP UNTIL THE STREETS RUN *RED WITH BLOOD!*

OR IF BLOOD IS UNAVAILABLE, THEN SWEAT, TEARS, OR A *GENERIC BLOOD SUBSTITUTE*.

SHELBYVILLE CITIZEN, ARISTOTLE AMADOPOLIS, DECLARED TODAY THAT UNLESS SPRINGFIELD *DISMANTLES* ITS ARSENAL BY *MIDNIGHT TONIGHT*, THEY WILL PLUNGE US INTO *FULL GLOBAL THERMONUCLEAR WAR*.

AS SEEN IN THAT REALLY COOL MATTHEW BRODERICK FILM.

MISSILE CRISIS

KENT

I'M SORRY IT HAD TO COME TO THIS, KENT, BUT WE'VE ALL LED LONG HAPPY LIVES, AND *I WILL NOT BACK DOWN!* DO YOUR WORST, ARI!

WE HERE AT CHANNEL 6 ADVISE YOU TO USE YOUR *REMAINING TIME* TO *MAKE PEACE* WITH YOUR *LOVED ONES*.

MISSIL

Sha-Boom Ka-Boom Cafe

LATER...

Millionaire's Club

$$$$$

NO
GAME SHOW
WINNERS ALLOWED

SIR! THE FIGHT IS OVER!

THE WINNER IS...

COAT CHECK

NOT NOW, SMITHERS! IS THAT THE *FINAL BID* FOR THE *WEAPONS STOCKPILE*? GOING, GOING...

...SOLD TO *HANK SCORPIO!*

WELL, THAT'S JUST *FANTASTIC.* YOU'VE *MADE* MY DAY! NO HARD FEELINGS, DR. COLOSSUS?

KILL SUPE

AAGH! WHAT A *WEEK* I'M HAVING!

DON'T YOU CARE WHO WON, SIR?

AH, SMITHERS, IN WAR THERE *ARE* NO WINNERS. THE ONLY *VICTORS* ARE THE *PEACE-MAKERS* AND THE *WAR PROFITEERS*.

WE WON, SIR.

EXCELLENT!

LATER...

WELL, I'M GLAD *THAT'S* OVER.

MOSTLY OVER. THE GOVERNMENT WAS SO *UPSET* AT AN *ATOMIC CIVIL WAR* BREAKING OUT BETWEEN *NEIGHBORING TOWNS* THAT THEY'VE *BANNED* THE CITY'S USE OF NUCLEAR MATERIALS FOR *SIX MONTHS.*

BUT WHERE WILL OUR *POWER* COME FROM?

REMEMBER ⋮GASP⋮ IF I HAVE *ANOTHER HEART ATTACK* ⋮WHEEZE⋮, WAKE ME FOR LUNCH!

WE REALLY NEED A BETTER UNION.

YOU NEVER FAIL TO AMAZE ME, SIR.

THANK YOU, SMITHERS. NOW WASH YOUR HANDS AND GET BACK IN YOUR WHEEL. YOUR *WOODCHIP BREAK* IS *OVER!*

THE END

HOMER VS. THE WALLPAPER

D'OH!

WHATCHA DOIN', HOMESLICE?

SPORT OF *KINGS*, MY BOY. I'M *HANGING* WALLPAPER!

I THOUGHT MOM GAVE YOU MONEY TO *HIRE* A PROFESSIONAL.

SCRIPT
NEIL ALSIP

PENCILS
JAMES LLOYD

INKS
TIM HARKINS

LETTERS
JEANNINE BLACK
JASON HO

COLORS
GUY INCOGNITO

EDITOR
BILL MORRISON

INTERIOR DESIGN
MATT GROENING

PROFESSIONALS! YOU KNOW WHAT PROFESSIONALS HAVE GOTTEN US?! THE TITANIC, THE ATOM BOMB, AND SUGAR SUBSTITUTES! *SOMEONE* HAS TO DRAW THE LINE AND *THAT* SOMEONE IS *ME!*

I'M GUESSING YOU *TOOK* THE MONEY AND SPENT IT ON *BEER.*

THAT'S NEITHER HERE NOR THERE.

RULE NUMBER ONE: ALWAYS MAKE SURE THE PASTE IS NEITHER TOO THIN NOR TOO THICK. THE BEST WAY TO FIND OUT IS THE BEST WAY TO FIND ANYTHING OUT...

HMM...NOT BAD, ALTHOUGH I FEEL A *STRANGE SENSATION*--

WALLPAPER GLU... NOW WITH 15% FEWER TOXIC FUMES!

AN HOUR AFTER THE *BOWEL DE-GLUING*...

NOW THAT WE HAVE *THAT* LITTLE UNPLEASANTNESS OUT OF THE WAY, IT'S TIME TO *CUT* THE WALLPAPER TO SIZE.

JUST *EVEN* IT UP A LITTLE...TAKE A *TEENSY* BIT OFF HERE...HMM... NOT QUITE EVEN. MAYBE A *PEENSY* BIT OFF THERE...

OKAY, THEN A TEENSY MORE *HERE*, PEENSY MORE *THERE*...STILL NOT RIGHT. TEENSY MORE...PEENSY MORE...*TEENSY!*... *PEENSY!*

YAAAARGH!!

NOW WE'LL SEE WHO'S BOSS!

Picture Perfect

WAIT! YOU'RE DARN RIGHT THERE'S BEEN A MISUNDERSTANDING! *I* PUT THAT THERE! THAT'S *MY* MARK! *I'M* THE ONE WHO MADE IT GREAT! *I* SHOULD GET THE $50! I UM, UH...

YOU'RE THE ONE WHO'S BEEN DOING THIS ALL OVER TOWN?

WELL, AT LEAST THAT MAKES SENSE.

ER...WAIT A MINUTE. HOW DO *YOU* KNOW I DID THE OTHER TAGS? MAYBE THIS IS A COPYCAT CRIME.

AARGHH! SOMEONE HAS DEFACED THE FRONT OF THE SCHYOOL! AND HE SIGNED HIS WORK, *BART SIMPSON!*

IT WASN'T ME! I WAS IN HERE DEFACING PROPERTY, NOT OUTSIDE. I DIDN'T DO THAT ONE!

IF I WAS NOT A MAN OF NON-VIOLENCE...OH, WHAT THE HECK, VISHNU WILL FORGIVE ME ON THIS ONE.

≡SIGH≡ I DIDN'T WIN WITH MY OWN WORK, AND BART GETS ALL THE ATTENTION. AGAIN.

NOW WAIT ONE MINUTE YOUNG LASS. AT LEAST YOU GOT THE PRIZE MONEY, AND HE GOT HIS COMEUPPANCE. AM I RIGHT?

HEY, THAT'S RIGHT. BUT HE COULDN'T HAVE EVEN DONE IT THIS TIME. I WONDER WHO GRAFFITIED THE SCHOOL?

DONTCHA WORRY YOUR PRETTY LITTLE HEAD ABOOT SUCH THINGS. NOW, WILLIE'S GOT SOME WORK TO DO.

THE END

STORY	PENCILS	INKS	LETTERS	COLORS	EDITOR	ART CRITIC
BILLY RUBENSTEIN	CHRIS HARMON	TIM BAVINGTON	KAREN BATES	CHRIS UNGAR	BILL MORRISON	MATT GROENING

SIEGE on EVERGREEN TERRACE

JESSE LEON MCANN
SCRIPT -

PHIL ORTIZ
PENCILS

TIM BAVINGTON
INKS

ART VILLANUEVA
COLORS

KAREN BATES
LETTERS

BILL MORRISON
EDITOR

MATT GROENING
TOWEL BOY

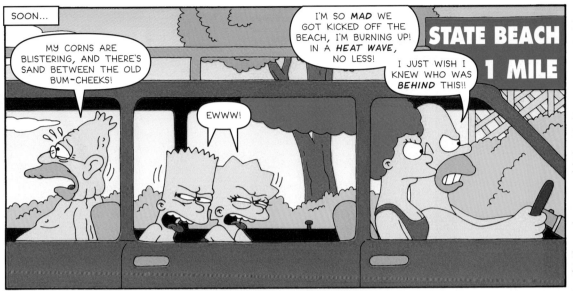

124

W-WELL, SIR, THE THING IS, *I* WAS SUPPOSED TO HAVE A POOL BUILT IN *MY* YARD WHILE I WAS GONE, AND THERE *DOESN'T* SEEM TO BE ONE THERE!

LISTEN FLANDERS, I CAN'T WORRY ABOUT THINGS THAT GO MISSING FROM *YOUR* YARD! YOU SHOULD CHAIN THINGS DOWN, LIKE I DO WITH MY *LAWN GNOMES*.

IT'S NOT THAT...

ARE YOU INFERRING THAT *THIS* IS YOUR POOL? WELL, IF THIS *WAS* YOUR POOL, WHAT WOULD IT BE DOING IN *MY* BACKYARD??

THAT'S WHAT *I'D* LIKE TO KNOW!

¡GASP!¿ IT'S CHUCK BLY...

...POOL GUY. YEAH, YEAH.

LISTEN BUDDY, YOU'VE *STOLEN* MR. FLANDERS POOL AND WE'RE TAKING IT *BACK*!

THAT IS, UNLESS YOU WANT TO *BUY* IT LEGALLY.

WHAT? HOW DARE YOU EMBARRASS ME IN FRONT OF MY *DISTINGUISHED* GUESTS?!

BESIDES, YOU CAN'T *REPOSSESS* A POOL.

NO, BUT WE *CAN* FILL IT IN! I'LL BE BACK WITH THE *DIRT TRUCKS*!

JUST WANTED TO CLEAR THAT UP! TOODLE-DOO!

I'D LIKE TO SEE YOU *TRY*! YOU'LL HAVE TO *BURY* ME FIRST!

OH, *NO*! WHAT AM I GOING TO DO?? I'VE GOT TO *THINK QUICK*!

133

WHAT TH...SOME-HOW HE'S *STILL GOT POWER!*

I MIGHT HAVE KNOWN! HE'S STEALING *YOUR POWER,* TOO!

ARE YOU SURE IT'S A GOOD IDEA TO TAKE AWAY THEIR *ELECTRICITY?*

THIS IS *PSYCHOLOGICAL WARFARE,* MR. FLANDERS, MEANT TO *WEED-OUT* THE WEAKLINGS. I WONDER WHO'LL BE THE FIRST TO *CRACK?*

AAAAAAAH! THE TV'S BLACKED-OUT AND THE BEER WILL GET WARM! WE'RE *DOOMED!!*

OOOOOH, FORGET IT! WE MIGHT AS WELL SURRENDER NOW!

ACTUALLY, I WAS JUST READING THE SIDE OF A WHEATIES BOX OUT LOUD.

GEE, DAD. YOU'RE NOT GIVING UP ARE YOU? YOU ALWAYS SAID THE ONLY FIGHTS WORTH WINNING WERE THE *HARD* FIGHTS.

YOU'RE FORGETTING, YOU ADULTS HAVE SOME-THING ON YOUR *SIDE* THAT THE CONSTRUCTION GUYS *DON'T--THE YOUTH OF AMERICA! WE'LL* HELP YOU BEAT THEM!

I'LL BE THE CAMP *TUNNEL RAT!*

EXCELLENT IDEA, MILHOUSE. DIG UNDER ENEMY LINES AND BRING US BACK SOME SUPPLIES.

MAKE SURE YOU GET MY DAD LOTS OF ICE FOR HIS BEER... AND *I'LL* HAVE ONE OF THOSE FINE *CUBAN CIGARS!*

YOU *GOT* IT!

138

THE END

"Duff Daddy!"

WRITTEN & DRAWN BY: *SCOTT SHAW!*
INKED BY: *TIM BAVINGTON*
COLORED BY: *CHRIS UNGAR*
LETTERED BY: *KAREN BATES*
EDITED BY: *BILL MORRISON*
BROUGHT TO YOU BY OUR PROUD SPONSOR: *MATT GROENING*

OKAY, PEOPLE, *SMOAKE & MEERERS* HAS GOTTA COME UP WITH A FRESH, *NEW AD CAMPAIGN* FOR THE *DUFF BEER* ACCOUNT!

MADISON AVE.

SO, ANY *SUGGESTIONS*, PEOPLE?

MAYBE IF WE INFERRED THAT *NOT* DRINKING DUFF BEER CAUSED *DANDRUFF*?

I DON'T THINK SO... AFTER ALL, *HONESTY* IS WHAT THE *ADVERTISING BUSINESS* IS ALL ABOUT!

WE NEED TO APPEAL TO THE *20 PER CENT* OF BEER BUYERS WHO ACCOUNT FOR OVER *80 PER CENT* OF ALL BEER SALES...

OR AS THE AGENCY LIKES TO CALL THEM, *"HEAVY USERS"*!

OR AS *I* LIKE TO CALL 'EM, *"ALCOHOLICS"*!

WE NEED THE OL' *"SLICE-OF-LIFE"* APPROACH! SOMETHING THAT THE *"JOE AVERAGE"* BEER DRINKER CAN RELATE TO!

ARE YOU *KIDDING*? BEER DRINKERS RELATE *ONLY* TO *BIG BOOBS* AND *TALKING ANIMALS*!

THAT'S IT! WE'LL CONDUCT A GRASSROOTS *TALENT SEARCH* TO FIND TWO *"TYPICAL"* DUFF DRINKERS.

ONE WHO'S A *BIG BOOB*!

AND ANOTHER ONE WHO LOOKS AND ACTS LIKE A *TALKING ANIMAL*!

AND WE'LL PIT ONE AGAINST THE OTHER, TRYING TO STEAL THE *DUFF BEER*! AFTER ALL, OUR FOCUS GROUP RESEARCH TELLS US THAT IF SOMETHING'S GOOD ENOUGH TO *STEAL*, IT *MUST* BE GOOD!

SO *WHY* ISN'T THE AGENCY APPLYING THAT THEORY TO OUR *CAR COMMERCIALS*?

GOOD *WORK*, PEOPLE! I *THINK* *SMOAKE* & *MEERERS* HAS ANOTHER *BIG HIT* ON ITS CORPORATE HANDS!

145

BRENT FLETCHER
SCRIPT

DAN DECARLO
LAYOUTS

MIKE DECARLO
PENCILS & INKS

KAREN BATES
COLORS & LETTERS

BILL MORRISON
EDITOR

MATT GROENING
CHAPERONE

SO, UH, JASMINE, WHAT DO YOU DO FOR A *LIVING*?

RIGHT NOW I'M WORKING AT TRY-N-SAVE. I'M TRYING TO *SKIM* ENOUGH MONEY FROM THE REGISTERS TO BUY A USED *MICROWAVE*.

RICK'S RIFLE RANGE

ALRIGHTY, DATERINO. THE FIRST THING THEY'VE GOT US DOING IS A LITTLE *SKEET SHOOTING*. HAVE YOU EVER SHOT A GUN BEFORE?

SURE. I *SHOOT* AT MY NEIGHBOR'S *DOGS* ALL THE TIME. I'M LOOKIN' TO MAKE ME A *FUR COAT*.

ENDORSED BY: CHARLTON HESTON OF THE NRA AND ALLEN IVERSON OF THE NBA

KNIFE THROWING

BEGINNERS

EXPERTS

NUGENTS

JUST LIKE AN EPISODE OF "THE A-TEAM."

THIS SEEMS LIKE GOOD, CLEAN FUN. IT'S A *LITTLE VIOLENT*, BUT WITHOUT ANY *BLOODSHED*.

MR. T SAYS, "I PITY THE FOOL ON THIS DATE!"

WELL I'LL BE A RIPE TURNIP! I SHOT THREE OUT OF FIVE!

YOU'RE A REGULAR ANNIE OAKLEY. NOW MOVE OVER *TWINKLE TOES*.

MY, YOU SEEM *AWFUL HANDY* WITH THAT SHOTGUN.

NUGENTS

I JUST CLOSE MY EYES AND LISTEN TO THE *VOICES IN MY HEAD*.

SO DID THE SON OF SAM, TED BUNDY, AND CHARLIE MANSON.

YOU KNOW, ACCORDING TO THIS DATING BOOK, YOU SHOULD BE IN THE *FRONT SEAT* WITH *ME!*

WELL, I USUALLY END UP IN THE *BACK SEAT*, SO I THOUGHT I'D SAVE SOME TIME!

DATING GUIDE

THIS PLACE LOOKS *FANCY*. HOLD ON WHILE I CHANGE INTO SOMETHING A LITTLE MORE APPROPRIATE.

The GILDED TRUFFLE

GUESS YOUR VALET'S BLOOD ALCOHOL LEVEL, WIN A *FREE* CAR DEODORIZER.

THIS PLACE HAS CLASS. *KENNY ROGERS-TYPE CLASS*. EVERYONE IS WEARING SHIRTS AND THE *SILVERWARE* AIN'T EVEN PLASTIC.

JASMINE TOLD BLIND LUCK SHE HAS EIGHT TATTOOS. WE CAN ONLY SEE TWO.

WHY DID WE HAVE TO STOP AT EVERY TABLE?

I WANTED THE PERFECT TABLE TO MAKE THIS THE MOST *ROMANTIC EVENING* EVER.

COULD WE GET SOME *SILVERWARE* HERE?

OUR SPECIAL TONIGHT IS A ROASTED DUCK LIGHTLY MARINATED IN VINAIGRETTE AND GARNISHED WITH BELGIAN CAPERS.

THAT SOUNDS GREAT. GO AHEAD AND *SUPER-SIZE* MINE.

THAT'S SIX GLASSES OF WINE. MAYBE YOU OUGHT TO *SLOW DOWN* A LITTLE.

SO YOU WANT TO ARM-WRESTLE?

NED SAYS HE'S NOT AFRAID TO TAKE AN OCCASIONAL RISK. ONCE A YEAR HE EATS THAI BBQ.

Velvet Blasphemy

LIVE DANCING

MOPING

NOW IT'S TIME FOR A LITTLE *DANCING*. WE SHOULDN'T HAVE TO WORRY ABOUT THIS *VIOLATING YOUR PAROLE*.

PAROLE SURE CAN BE *TOUGH*. THERE ARE DAYS I FEEL LIKE I CAN'T BE WITHIN *FIVE-HUNDRED YARDS* OF ANYONE!

EISNER AWARD WINNER!

SIMPSONS COMICS

#56

US $2.50
CAN $3.50

© & TM BONGO ENTERTAINMENT, INC. THE SIMPSONS © & TM TWENTIETH CENTURY FOX FILM CORPORATION. ALL RIGHTS RESERVED.

THE
YES-MAN
WHO WOULD BE
King

DOUG TUBER,
TIM MAILE,
STEVE LUCHSINGER
SCRIPT

JOHN COSTANZA
PENCILS

TIM BAVINGTON
INKS

ART VILLANUEVA
COLORS

KAREN BATES
LETTERS

BILL MORRISON
EDITOR

MATT GROENING
MONARCH OF MIRTH

I'LL WING MY TOPPER ONTO YOUR LEFT, OR *SINISTER*, HAND, SNATCH MY OPERA HAT, AND BE OFF TO THE *THEATER!*

OOF!

EXCELLENT TOSS, SIR. I COULD TELL YOU WERE *AIMING* FOR THAT FLOOR TILE.

PLOP!

MY AIM WAS PUT OFF BY THE *RAZOR-SHARP STEEL* I HAD INSERTED IN THE BRIM. WEIGHS ME DOWN, BUT IT'LL MAKE A DANDY *SURPRISE* FOR THE NEXT *ROUGHNECK* LOOKING TO *WAYLAY* ME.

WELL DONE, SMITHERS. YOU MAKE A FINE SUBSTITUTE *HAT RACK.*

WHEN WILL YOUR ELEPHANT-IVORY HAT-RACK COME BACK FROM THE *POLISHER'S*, SIR?

TOMORROW. SO I'LL NEED YOU TO STAND HERE *ALL NIGHT*. AND DON'T MOVE--I DON'T LIKE IT WHEN HAT RACKS MOVE, UNLESS THEY'RE FEATURED IN A *MUSICAL NUMBER* IN A *JOLLY CARTOON.*

I'LL BE HERE, SIR. NOT MOVING.

BUT A HAT RACK CAN ALWAYS *DREAM*...

"SMITHERS! WHERE ARE YOU?"

HUH?

SMITHERS, COME HERE! I *NEED YOU!*

IT'S MORNING! I MUST HAVE DOZED OFF!

I'M HERE, SIR. DON'T UPSET YOURSELF. YOU'RE PRONE TO *VAPORS!*

I COULDN'T SLEEP LAST NIGHT, SO I WATCHED "THE MAKING OF 'I'LL TAKE SWEDEN.'" THAT ANITA EKBERG IS QUITE A *DISH*. CONSEQUENTLY, I HAVE A *YEN* FOR *SWEDISH FOOD*. SCAMPER DOWN TO *LITTLE STOCKHOLM* AND FETCH ME SOME ROLLMOPS, HERRING-MIT-BROD AND AQUAVIT.

I'LL BE BACK BEFORE YOU CAN SAY "KALHYGGEN OCH FORBRANNING," SIR!

SOON, IN THE SECTION OF SPRINGFIELD KNOWN AS *LITTLE STOCKHOLM*...

VOLVO REPAIR and Sauna

VOLVO

SKOLL! LITTLE STOCKHOLM! SPRINGFIELD'S HIGHEST SUICIDE RATE! PARKING FREE WITH VALIDATION!

HELD OVER 1,807TH WEEK SCENES FROM A MARRIAGE

Stewardess School and Sauna

SMORGASBORD and SAUNA

HMMM, I HAVE THE *FLATBROD* AND THE *AQUAVIT*. CAN'T FIND THE *GRAVLAX*...

STOCK UP ON STOCKHOLM STOCKINGS

MAX VON SYDOW NUTCRACKERS

DEATH TO DANDRUFF Shampoo

CAN I HELP YOU FIND SOMETHING?

I CAN'T FIND GRAVLAX. HOW CAN THERE BE *MEANING IN LIFE*?

THERE IS NO MEANING. ALL LIFE IS AN *AGONY* OF WINTER WINDS AND *SORROW*. BUT SMOKED FISH IS ON AISLE THREE.

:GASP!:

BY THE BEARD OF CRAFTY ODIN, FATHER GOD OF NEIGHBORING NORWAY...

...THE RESEMBLANCE IS UNCANNY!

OPERATOR, GET ME NORSE-SIDE 777.

HELLO, *SWEDISH EMBASSY*?

156

...AND A HERRING-AND-WATERCRESS SALAD WHICH TOOK ME *TWO HOURS* TO MAKE.

I'VE CHANGED MY MIND. I WANT SOMETHING MORE *RO-BUST* FOR BREAKFAST. *STEAK AND EGGS* SHOULD BE JUST WHAT THE DOCTOR ORDERED.

OF COURSE, I'LL NEED YOU TO *CHEW IT UP* AND *REGURGITATE* IT FOR ME. I'LL WAIT.

DING-♪ ♪ DONG!

CAN I HELP YOU?

OLAV GUSTAVSON, MASTER OF HERALDRY FOR THE ROYAL HOUSE OF SWEDEN.

INGA CARLSDOTTIR, PROFESSOR OF GENE-OLOGY, UNIVERSITY OF GOTEBORG.

GRETTA LILLQUIST, DEEP-TISSUE MASSAGE, IN-CALL, OUT-CALL.

MR. SMITHERS, THE CURRENT *KING OF SWEDEN* IS AT *DEATH'S DOOR*, MAKING ME SAD.

HEH, HEH. *ANOTHER* OLD FOE I'VE *OUT-LIVED!*

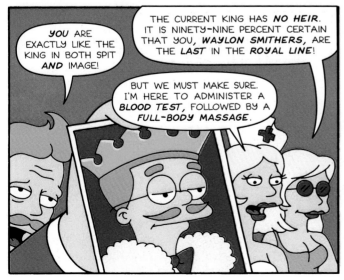

YOU ARE EXACTLY LIKE THE KING IN BOTH SPIT *AND* IMAGE!

THE CURRENT KING HAS *NO HEIR.* IT IS NINETY-NINE PERCENT CERTAIN THAT YOU, *WAYLON SMITHERS,* ARE THE *LAST* IN THE *ROYAL LINE!*

BUT WE MUST MAKE SURE. I'M HERE TO ADMINISTER A *BLOOD TEST,* FOLLOWED BY A *FULL-BODY MASSAGE.*

I MIGHT BE THE KING OF SWEDEN?

SOON, ALL OVER TOWN...

...THAT WAYLON SMITHERS MIGHT BE THE REAL KING OF SWEDEN!

WELL, *HE* WON'T BE PRODUCING ANY HEIRS.

...SO HE'D PROBABLY GET TO LIVE IN A *BIG PALACE!*

...SERVANTS CATERING TO HIS *EVERY WHIM!*

...PAINTING DWARVES GOLD AND USING 'EM AS LIFE-SIZED CHESS PIECES!

...INDOOR HORSE-RACING, NAKED TWISTER, DOGS DRESSED LIKE PEOPLE!

...A WHOLE ROOM MADE OF BEEF JERKY. FURNITURE, CARPET, EVERY-THING! AND A LAKE MADE OF BEER AND A STAFF TO ROW YOU AROUND WHILE YOU DRINK!

AND THEY'RE WELL-NIGH *SLAVES!* IT'S HOW HE DOES WI' EVERYONE. AND IF YA DISAGREE--THEY CLAP YA IN IRONS AN' INTAE THE DUNGEON WI' YE!

PROPERTY SEIZURES! BEATINGS! RANDOM ARRESTS! TORTURE! JUST LIKE HOME.

TODAY I SAW A CLOUD THAT LOOKED LIKE A CHOO-CHOO!

I HEAR WAYLON SMITHERS MIGHT BE THE REAL KING OF SWEDEN!

HEH, HEH. YOU AND YOUR STORIES.

159

MR. BURNS, I WAS TOLD YOU WANT TO SEE ME. I'M SORRY I ACCIDENT-ALLY RELEASED *RADIOACTIVE WASTE* INTO THE CITY'S *WATER SUPPLY!*

GOOD LORD, YOU REALLY *DID* THAT?

YES, I DI--UM... I MEAN...THAT IS...WHAT DID YOU WANT TO SEE ME ABOUT?

MY NEW ROYAL FRIEND HERE REQUIRES A STAFF OF LACKEYS, BOOT-LICKS AND CHURLS. SO, I'VE BEEN THINKING...

SOON...

EXCELLENT! BUT LET'S HAVE THE CHAMBER-MAID AND THE WIZARD *SWITCH UNIFORMS.*

HOMER, I'M NOT SURE PULLING THE KIDS OUT OF SCHOOL SO THEY CAN BE *SERVANTS* IS THE BEST IDEA.

AND I WOULD AGREE WITH YOU, MARGE, IF IT WASN'T FOR *THREE* LITTLE WORDS..."*SMOR-GAS-BORD!*" IF WE LIVE IN SWEDEN WE MAY NOT BE KINGS, BUT WE CAN *EAT* LIKE THEM!

THERE'S YOUR *ROYAL RETINUE,* YOUR HIGHNESS. ENJOY!

I WILL! A FELLOW COULD REALLY GET USED TO THE ROYAL TREATMENT...

OCH! AND YE CALL YERSELF A *KING*! A KING SHOULD STAND SIX FEET TALL AND WEIGH TWENTY STONE. YER NOTHING BUT A *SPECTACLE-WEARIN' COUF* WITH A SHELF FULL O' MALIBU STACY DOLLS.

AND YOU CERTAINLY DON'T DISPLAY THE SORT OF TEMPERATE, LAW-GIVING WISDOM OF, FOR INSTANCE, A CHUCK HESTON.

NO, UNTIL I SEE SOME CRACKER-JACK *PROCLAMATION MAKING* AND THE OCCASIONAL HEAVY-HANDED *DEATH SENTENCE*, I'LL SAVE *MY ALLEGIANCE* FOR *JESSE "THE BODY" VENTURA*.

HMMM...I REALLY *HAVEN'T* PROVED THAT I DESERVE TO BE KING...THERE MUST BE *SOMETHING* I CAN DO.

I ASKED HER OUT FIRST!

LISTEN, ER, AH, NEWSBOY, *I* SAW MISS SCISSORS FIRST, AND *I'M* TAKING HER OUT!

FELLAS, FELLAS!

MAYBE *I* CAN SETTLE THIS. I DO HAVE *KINGLY WISDOM*, AFTER ALL.

WE'LL HAVE MISS SCISSORS STAND INSIDE THIS CIRCLE. THEN YOU EACH GRAB ONE OF HER ARMS, AND WHOEVER PULLS HER OUT GETS TO *DATE* HER.

YOU SEE, WHOEVER *REALLY CARES* ABOUT THIS WOMAN WON'T PULL ON HER ARM, TO AVOID *HURTING* HER.

HEH, HEH. JUDICIOUS *AND* A SEXY SPECTACLE.

WORD OF SMITHERS' WISDOM QUICKLY SPREADS, AND SOON...

KRUSTY'S FENCE IS THREE FEET ONTO MY PROPERTY. I WANT TO BUILD A TOOL SHED THERE. HE SHOULD *MOVE* THAT FENCE.

WHEN I *BUILT* THAT FENCE, SAW-BONES HERE AGREED IT WAS ON THE *PROPERTY LINE!* I *NEED* THAT SPACE NOW. I GOT MY *IN-LAWS* BURIED THERE!

DR. HIBBERT, BUILD YOUR SHED ON *STILTS*. THAT WAY, KRUSTY'S FAMILY STAYS BURIED, YOU CAN HAVE YOUR TOOL SHED, AND A *LOVELY VIEW* TO BOOT.

SOUNDS FAIR TO ME.

AS LONG AS I CAN KEEP MY MOTHER-IN-LAW WHERE SHE IS. THE *TOMATOES* I PLANTED ON TOP OF HER ARE COMING IN LIKE *GANGBUSTERS!*

...SO, SUPERINTENDENT CHALMERS THOUGHT HE WAS BUYING *MATH TEXTBOOKS*, AND WHAT MR. LEGS SOLD HIM WAS, IN FACT, *CIGARETTES* AND *JAPANESE EROTICA*. I DECREE THAT MR. LEGS SUPPLY THE TEXTBOOKS, FOR *HALF* THE ORIGINAL PRICE.

THAT'S VERY WISE AND JUDICIOUS, AND I'LL TAKE THE EROTICA IF NO ONE ELSE WANTS IT.

BECAUSE WAYLON SMITHERS DISPLAYS WISDOM AND ASSORTED QUALITIES OF LEADERSHIP UNRELATED TO *GRAFT* AND *WOMANIZING,* I HEREBY *DEFER* ALL *CIVIC AUTHORITY* TO HIM. *ALL HAIL KING WAYLON!*

MR. SMITHERS IS A *GODSEND* FROM OUR MANY GODS!

HE'LL TELL US HOW TO LIVE!

HE'S THE *BEST* THING TO HAPPEN TO THIS TOWN SINCE "CREAMED WEENIE WEDNESDAYS" AT KRUSTY BURGER!

EXCUSE ME, BUT WE SHOULD THINK TWICE BEFORE WE *HAND OVER* COMPLETE AUTHORITY TO ANY *ONE MAN.* WE LIVE IN A SYSTEM OF *CHECKS AND BALANCES* TO PREVENT THE *TYRANNY* WHICH INEVITABLY FLOWS FROM *ABSOLUTE POWER.*

SHE'S TRYING TO KEEP US FREE. *DESTROY HER!*

GET THE LITTLE GIRL!

I LOVE LISA, BUT SHE HAS TO STOP LIVING!

HOLD ON! THIS IS MY LITTLE *DAUGHTER!* SHE'S *PRECIOUS!* LET'S JUST *TAR AND FEATHER* HER AND *RUN HER OUT OF TOWN.*

HURRY, LISA. *HIDE!*

THANKS, MOM. I'LL ALWAYS REMEMBER YOU.

AND SO, SMITHERS' WORD WAS LAW THROUGHOUT THE LAND!

WHAT A *SHAMEFUL SPECTACLE*. A SIGHT LIKE THAT IS A BLOT ON OUR TOWN.

HENCEFORTH, I DECREE THAT ALL BUMS AND BEGGARS BE PROVIDED WITH SMART WARDROBES AND FREE HAIR GROOMING!

HUZZAH!

EXERCISE ISN'T ONLY GOOD FOR YOUNG PEOPLE, IT'S GOOD FOR EVERYONE.

I HEREBY ORDAIN THAT FOR TWO HOURS EVERY AFTERNOON, EACH CITIZEN OF SPRINGFIELD WILL EITHER ROLLER BLADE, ICE DANCE, OR "SWEAT TO THE OLDIES!"

ICE DANCING! *HOORAY!*

TOMORROW MORNING, *AMC* IS SHOWING "ALL ABOUT EVE" IN ITS *"DAMES WE LOVE" SERIES!* I DECLARE THIS A *CIVIC HOLIDAY*, AND EVERY MAN, WOMAN AND CHILD IS REQUIRED TO SAVOR BETTE DAVIS AND CELESTE HOLME IN *THE MOST OUTRAGEOUS CATFIGHT OF THE CENTURY!*

HMMM...

I'M ALL FOR CATTY *GIRL-FIGHTING* ON THE SILVER SCREEN, BUT CLOSING THE SCHOOLS STRIKES ME AS RATHER *HIGH-HANDED*.

YE CAN SAY THAT AGAIN. WE'RE ONE STEP AWA' FROM *RE-EDUCATION CAMPS* AND *FORCED BREEDIN'* BETWEEN STATE-SELECTED COUPLES.

PSST!

SPRINGFIELD FREE FOREVER!

CLEARLY, OUR FIRST PRIORITY IS A PLAN OF ACTION TO *ELIMINATE* MR. SMITHERS' TYRANNY. IDEAS?

I THINK WE NEED TO CHANGE OUR *SLOGAN*. THERE'S NO VERB. AS IT'S WRITTEN, "FREE" IS ADJECTIVAL.

I'D LIKE SOMETHING THAT INVOKES THE CREATOR, TO ENSURE DIVINE BENEDICTION ON OUR UPCOMING MAYHEM.

TO *MY* MIND, A LOGO IS NAE A LOGO IF IT DINNA SHOW A ROYAL GETTIN' HIS PONCEY SKULL BATTERED IN WI' A JAGGED ROCK.

I THINK THERE SHOULD BE AN ELEPHANT.

CAN WE FOCUS ON OUR GOAL, PLEASE?

WAIT! WE HAVEN'T HEARD FROM MR. TEENY, YET.

EEEK! YAP! EEEH-EEEH-EEEH!

THANK YOU, MR. TEENY. AS WE KNOW, THE BLOOD TESTS WILL BE IN ON SATURDAY. SMITHERS WILL BE KING OF SWEDEN, AND SPRINGFIELD HAS ALREADY AGREED TO BECOME A *SWEDISH PROTECTORATE*.

SMITHERS' CORONATION PRO-CESSION WILL PASS RIGHT OVER THESE CATACOMBS!

I PROPOSE WE *KID-NAP* SMITHERS AND *SET HIM ADRIFT*. HE'LL FLOAT TO SEA, WHERE HE CAN BE TAKEN TO SWEDEN. SPRINGFIELD WILL NEVER LOSE ITS LIBERTY.

SEEMS FINE.

I AGREE WITH THAT.

I VOTE "AYE," WITH THE WEE CHANGE THAT WE USE AN OAR TO BATTER HIS BRAINS INTO PASTE.

NOW, LET'S GET OUT O' HERE-- THIS PLACE HAS A MIGHTY STINK.

IF YOU WANT TO BUY A PAT BOONE CD, THAT'S FINE. YOU DON'T NEED MY PERMISSION.

DANDY!

THAT'S ALL FOR TODAY. THE KING NEEDS HIS REST.

ANYBODY WANNA GO TO LITTLE STOCK-HOLM FOR MEATBALLS AND LINGONBERRIES?

I HEAR THEY'VE GOT A PORTRAIT OF KING WAYLON DONE ENTIRELY IN RANUNCULUS.

NAW, I'M GONNA GO WANDER THROUGH THE NEW MUNICIPAL FLOWER GARDEN.

LET'S GET HIS MAJESTY BACK INSIDE.

CAN WE GET YOU ANYTHING? ROYAL SLIPPERS? ROYAL APPLE JUICE? ROYAL CROWN COLA?

NO, THANK YOU. LEAVE ME ALONE, THANK YOU.

IT'S *LONELY* BEING KING. NO ONE TO *CONFIDE* IN. NO ONE TO SHARE WITH. NO ONE TO TAKE TO A MIDNIGHT SHOWING OF "HAIRSPRAY."

I DON'T LIKE CHICKEN. SIMPSON, COME HERE.

NO...MORE...CHICKEN! *EVER!* I WANT *CONDOR! CONDOR CUTLETS!*

AND THAT SHOULD BE *ME* GETTING A PERFECTLY GOOD DINNER MASHED IN MY FACE DURING AN *INFANTILE TEMPER TANTRUM.*

I CAN STAND DISPENSING ROYAL JUSTICE. I CAN SURVIVE LIVING IN WEALTH AND SPLENDID ISOLATION...

BUT I'M GOING TO MISS BEING A *SPINELESS LICKSPITTLE* TO THAT *MAGNIFICENT MAN.*

THE NEXT DAY...

ALL HAIL KING WAYLON...
AND *IN*HALE LARAMIE CIGARETTES!

MR. SMITHERS, I HAVE THE RESULTS OF YOUR BLOOD TESTS.

I'M A BIT TIED UP RIGHT NOW. I'LL LOOK AT THEM LATER.

TAN TAN TARRA!

THEY'RE COMING. GET READY TO *GRAB* MR. SMITHERS. FIVE... FOUR...

"THREE..."

WHIRR...

"TWO..."

CLICK!

WHUH...?

THE END